THE FATHER'S BLESSING

Healing the Father Wound

THE FATHER'S BLESSING

Healing the Father Wound

PAUL TESKE

DALLAS, TX

Paul Teske Ministries

Dallas, TX 75219

The Father's Blessing: Healing the Father Wound

by Paul Teske

Printed in the United States of America.

International Standard Book Number:
978-1-7379051-0-3 (Print)
978-1-7379051-1-0 (e-Book)
978-1-7379051-2-7 (Audiobook)

CONTENTS

DEDICATION

I dedicate this book first and foremost to The Triune God- Father, Son and Holy Spirit. May God receive all glory, honor, praise, and thanks.

Secondly, to my beloved wife, Rivers, who has stood by my side through thick and thin while never flinching. She has followed me around the world and remains my most trusted confidant and dearest best friend.

Thirdly, to my wonderful children, their spouses, and my grandchildren. They enabled me to pour out my love and affirm them as my beloved sons and daughters.

Lastly, I dedicate this book to all the men and women who have received the Father's Blessing through our ministry, and for those yet to be set free through this ministry.

ENDORSEMENTS

The Enemy's most effective attack on God and all God loves has been to attack fathers and fatherhood. Because of the utter centrality of fathers, everything and everyone is affected. Therefore there is literally nothing more important than healing the "father wounds" in millions of hearts around the world – and this book shows you how! Please read this book and share it with all who need it.

— Eric Metaxas, #1 NY Times Bestselling author of Bonhoeffer, Martin Luther, and Miracles.

Paul Teske has been a dear friend of mine since 2007. I have had the privilege of meeting some of God's dearest friends and most trusted servants over the years. I can honestly say that Paul is a gift to the world, the body of Christ and to me personally. He loves Jesus and people faithfully. I am honored to call him a friend and vital voice in my life. I pray this book blesses you and your family, as you discover how wonderful our Heavenly Father is.

—Michael Koulianos, Pastor and Founder of Jesus Image

In the New Testament we hear these words, "How great is the love the Father has lavished on us, that we should be called children of God! And that is what we are!" (1 John 3:1) Sadly, too many people do not experience real love from their own earthly fathers and, therefore, live life as walking wounded. In this excellent book, Paul Teske shows us that we are loved lavishly by our heavenly Father and how we can find healing in Him. He also teaches dads important lessons about passing on God's lavish love to their children. A must read for parents.

—Tim Runtsch, Lead Pastor at Redeemer Church in Fort Collins and Greeley, Colorado

The Father's blessing powerfully changed my life. I was a man in my 60s, a Jesus follower, father to five grown children and seven grandchildren, but I still sensed a void of what my earthly father could never give me. Paul Teske put his arms around me and spoke the fathers blessing over me. There was no emotional experience at that moment, but the next day I woke up changed. I had a new foundation knowing that God loved me, that He accepted me, and that He was even pleased with me. Now I can build upon that foundation. Since then, I have given this blessing to my children for them to pass on to their children. This book gives deeper understanding how important it is for fathers to give their blessing and unconditional love to their children. "He will turn the hearts of the parents to their children, and the hearts of the children to their parents; or else I will come and strike the land with total destruction."

Malachi 4:6 NIV

—Robbie Briggs, CEO of Briggs Freeman Sotheby's International Realty, Dallas, Texas.

The Father's Blessing is a truly great book by a truly great pastor and author! Paul Teske, guided by the Spirit of God, has put his finger on a place of great pain and vulnerability in our world. Through this wonderful teaching, he helps each of us discover freedom and peace ... healing for our hearts and minds ... through the Father's Blessing.

> —*Bill Tucker, Senior Pastor, Concordia Lutheran Church, San Antonio, Texas*

I wish I had this book prior to my own healing journey on Father wounds .It is so important to think deeply on what the Holy Spirit is saying to you though Rev Paul Teske's teaching on this issue of our heart formation. Healing of the Father wound will effect every area of your life, I have been on site, watching and praying as Rev Paul Teske moves with God's healing with many people and know the teaching in his book is deeply needed.

> —*Lorna Dueck – CEO, Crossroads/YES TV (Canada) and Host of Context Beyond the Headlines*

This book is Full of the Holy Spirit who guides us into all truth. Full of God's word which does not return void. Full of compassion, peace and mercy which is who Jesus was on this earth and in Heaven. Jesus is a miracle worker and still performs miracles all the time but sometimes the miracles are evident for all to see and sometimes they are deep within us and can even be more miraculous than the physical! The good news is the inner healing of one's heart then manifests in the physical healing which is easy for God!

This revelation God gave to Paul Teske of the Fathers Blessing is transformative for personal lives and lives of families that can then operate healed and whole, whether their father is still on this earth or not!

God always heals, always restores always redeems but we often need the tools to discover that, and this book does just that! Thanks to Paul for his faithful obedience to his Lord and Savior to put these truths into our hands to discover our brokenness and how God can fill the broken places with His Love, the ultimate Fathers Love.

—*Heather Washburne*
Dallas, Texas

FOREWORD

I have had the privilege to know Rev. Paul Teske for the last twelve years as a spiritual father, mentor, teacher, and friend. I first met him over a phone call in the spring of 2008 as I was asking for his help with a pastor friend of mine. I never imagined that that one call would take me into a new world and deeper understanding of the Holy Spirit, Jesus, and our Heavenly Father.

Pastor Paul started traveling from his church in Connecticut to my home in Dallas to teach my home group on the gifts of the Holy Spirit. During this time, His book on healing, Healing for Today was published. It is a must read for Christian men and women wishing to move in God's healing power or seeking healing from our Lord. His own healing testimony has moved too many to count. During this season, we saw wonderful evidence of Jesus' love and will to heal and move in His children's lives.

I believe that the best is still ahead for Rev. Teske; this book about the Father's Blessing and the healing of our father wounds will be a world changer. The Father's Blessing is a lost Biblical practice that needs to be taught, learned, and practiced in our homes and churches. This book helps establish the biblical history, personal need, and practical methods of giving and receiving the Father's Blessing.

My own father died suddenly at 63 years old when I was in my late 30s and, though he told me many times that he loved me and was proud of me, there were many tough years as he battled alcoholism and his own father wounds. When I was 25 years old, I led a family intervention that was the catalyst for him to never have another drink. Childhood wounds can be deep and lasting and, though we had tough times early in my life, we made wonderful progress to find healing together.

Though my Dad was a man of faith and his love for Jesus grew as he matured, if either of us had known the power of a father's blessing, we both would have got ours. I would have loved to hear what blessings he would have spoken over me. I would have also wondered how such a blessing would have impacted the destiny of my life if I hadn't received one from Rev. Teske 10 years ago when he stood in the place of my earthly father. On that day, Pastor Paul asked me many questions about my father, our relationship, and any issues or unforgiveness that I might still be holding.

Pastor Paul asked if he could speak for my earthly father. I said, "Yes!" He began to tell me all the things every little boy or girl wants to hear from a father. In his arms his voice actually sounded like my Father's deep voice and he told me that he loved me and why he did. I began to cry...hard. He then told me that he was proud of me and why he was, but the most impactful moment was when he asked me to forgive him for anything he said, did or did not do that hurt me or made me feel less valuable. Though I thought I had settled any forgiveness issues with my father long ago, I was barely able to get out the words of my forgiveness. I felt like I was having a moment with my father and I told him that I missed him and love him. He proceeded to bless me with blessings that every man would desire.

I know my father was in God's throne room on that day and I believe was allowed to share with the Holy Spirit many of those same words about how he felt about me that Paul spoke. Those words sunk deep into my soul and brought freedom and joy.

I hope you dig deeply into this book and learn how to receive and give a father's blessing. If your father is still living, maybe you will be able to ask and receive this blessing from him. If it is not possible for any reason, I hope you will allow God to raise up a father figure like the Lord did for me in Pastor Teske. I hope you will let that man stand in for your father and speak love and forgiveness into your life.

I also hope that this book will inspire you to bless your children, heal any lingering wounds, and speak the holy power of God's love, forgiveness, and blessings into their lives.

I have given this father's blessing to my own children and many other adults and young adults over the years. I have seen healing of physical issues as well as emotional and spiritual ones. I pray that this waits for you and may our Lord Jesus receive all the glory.

G. Hugh Brandon

INTRODUCTION

I believe that the most powerful relationship in a person's life is with his or her father. This relationship is the key to living a successful and prosperous life or a life shaped by striving, struggle, and emptiness of the soul. As I minister to people, I always ask them about their relationship to their father (biological, adopted, step, or multiple) with a series of questions. My motive is to ascertain the relationship between a person and his father.

What was your relationship with your father like?

The response to this question runs the gamut from:

"He was awesome!"

"He was average."

"He was abusive."

"He was angry."

"He was absent."

Did your father love you?

The responses to this question are equally revealing:

"Yes."

"I think so?"

"Sometimes."

"Depends."

"I don't know."

"No!"

Did your father ever say to you, "I love you"?

A few say:

"Yes."

Most say:

"No."

"No, but I know he loved me."

"No, because…"

If your relationship with your earthly father was not good, then this book is for you. My desire is to guide you to a place of spiritual affirmation as a man or woman so you can be healed from the deep wound in your heart caused by your earthly father. This healing will bring safety and an ability to trust your Heavenly Father. The way a person perceives his or her earthly father will most often determine the way he sees his Heavenly Father. I believe you can have a supernatural restoration with your father and with your Heavenly Father. I know you are sick and tired of being "sick and tired," but healing for the father wound is on the way!

Secondly, if you had a stellar, awesome, and amazing relationship with your earthly father, then that is wonderful. I celebrate that for you. But I know that you are aware of someone who was deeply wounded by their father and needs restoration. You can guide them to a place of healing in their heart and help them secure trust with their Heavenly Father.

The antidote to the father wound is the Father's Blessing—both from your natural father and your Heavenly Father. This blessing will supernaturally heal your father wound.

Prologue

AN EMPTY CELL

Several years ago, I accepted a conference invitation to speak to a group of millennials about my personal ministry and travels. At the end of my talk, I ordered a cappuccino at the coffee station in the atrium and overheard a young man sharing about his conversion to Christianity while in prison. As the small group disbursed, I approached the young man who appeared to be in his mid-thirties and introduced myself. As we talked, I could tell from his demeanor that he was introverted and extremely guarded. After a few more minutes of small talk, I shared that I had heard him say he had become a Christian in prison and asked if he could tell me more about his intriguing story. He told me that he was released several years earlier from federal prison for good behavior and, while there, had found a new relationship with Jesus. As he shared, I felt a divine connection in my spirit.

As he started speaking with a measured amount of caution, he nervously told me he had grown up as an only child to working parents. His mother worked locally, and his father often travelled for work. From an early age, he would find himself alone at home to fend for himself. His adolescence was shaped by peers who helped him experience a variety of things including pornography, cigarettes, alcohol, and drugs. At first, his escape from the painful reality of his parentless life was marijuana, to which he became hooked. Later, he grew dependent on harder drugs. The cost was more than he could afford, which led, of course, to stealing and eventually selling off household goods from unsuspecting parents.

In high school, he discovered his innate knack for business when he made a substantial profit selling drugs. As he entered his college years, he was able to network his sales and drug distribution through other college students he knew in the surrounding states. The outward facade shouted college success to his parents: he was invincible, and the sky was the limit! At this point in the story, his tone had shifted from apprehension to full throttled confidence and pride in his accomplishments. Suddenly, his face clearly displayed the depth of the misfortune to follow. He took a deep breath and paused for a moment as though he was at a loss for words. Tears streamed down his face. Remorse? Regret? Disappointment? I sat and waited for him to gather his thoughts, praying in silence. I knew at that moment the fruit of this divine appointment was about to manifest. I stood up and walked over to the coffee bar for a napkin, brought it back, and gave it to him. As he wiped away the tears, he apologized for becoming emotional. We locked eyes for a moment and then he continued to share his story.

Then one day, the crash came. The FBI made an early morning raid on his apartment. Because he was transporting drugs for sale across state lines, several federal crimes had been committed. As a result, he was convicted and sent to federal prison for several years. He shared that his initial and early prison experience was harsh and dark as he tried to isolate himself as much as possible. He said that he lived in absolute terrorizing fear for his life. He was raised in a middle-class home where life was safe, or so he thought. Now he lived amongst a criminal element of society where he knew his life had virtually no value whatsoever. He shared that he would cry out to God (even though he did not really know how to pray) and waited in the quiet silence of his cell for a response that never came. Or so he thought.

Eventually he made his way to the chapel one day where he met the prison chaplain. The chaplain encouraged him emotionally and extended a friendly invitation to attend Sunday services. A few weeks later, the chaplain invited him to a weekly Bible study where he met other inmates. He silently listened to their stories and testimonies about how and when they had "met" Jesus and accepted Him as Lord and Savior. He would return to his cell and think through each narrative and inwardly long to have that kind of encounter, to change his own life. Inwardly he yearned for love, peace, joy, and hope. He felt so empty and longed to be filled up with what they had. He was never the "tough guy" like other inmates tried to be, but distant, guarded, lonely, empty, and ready.

During one of the Bible studies, the chaplain had turned to him and pointedly asked about how he felt. He said it was like a dam that had burst open. Even though he fought to control his emotions, he could not hold back the tears that came. That day, he confessed his need for Jesus and received Him into his life. Everything changed. He began to fervently read the Bible the chaplain had given him earlier and felt like a sponge, absorbing every word he read. He became more engaged in his faith, prayer life, even worship opportunities. He could not get enough of God.

The day finally arrived when he was released from prison. He decided that he needed to find a good Bible-based church in his town. His chaplain helped him plug into a local church family with a great mentoring pastor. He shared with me that his current employment was sufficient and that he was considering ministry of some sort, but did not know "where, when, or how" that would happen.

While sharing his life saga with me, we had moved to a sitting area with our coffee to be more comfortable. The more we talked, the more at ease he was to share personal issues with me. When he had finished telling me his story, I asked him a question: "What was your father like?" Without any hesitation as I asked, he blurted, "Terrible!" He did not seem angry or disgusted, just apathetic —emotionally void. I asked him, "Did he ever say he loved you?" He looked at me as though he was confused and uncertain of what I meant. He quietly murmured, "NO!"

Our focus turned into a lengthy discourse about his father who had never affirmed him, hugged him, told him he was proud of him, or engaged in any activity with him. My new friend shared with me that, if his father was not absent, he was berating, belittling, criticizing, mocking, demeaning, condescending, and degrading. He said his father was never physically abusive, but verbally vicious to both him and his mother. He said he could never understand why his mother put up with his father's cruelty. He concluded that maybe he and his mother shared the common denominator of living in the father's lengthy absences as just enough motivation to stick it out. There really was no place to go, as he thought through the situation. He hated it when his father was home.

At the end of his lengthy narrative, I paused for a few seconds and then looked straight into his eyes and asked if he had honestly ever forgiven his father? He stared at me as though I were speaking a foreign language. He dropped his head. He said nothing. I continued, "Forgiveness is actually the key to spiritual freedom and the pathway to establishing a relationship of trust with the Heavenly Father." I knew the real freedom my young friend needed.

I asked him if he could fully and completely trust God and he reluctantly offered a "yes." I asked him if I could pray for him to receive an impartation of the Father's love and he gave me an affirmative nod.

We both stood up. I put my arms around him and held him tightly in my arms in a bear hug. I said "I am going to speak as your father by name," which I did. I proceeded to speak as his father, asking his forgiveness for the vast inventory of deep wounds inflicted over his lifetime. There were moments when he wanted to push me back, but I continued to hold him close and tight. Speaking as his father, I relentlessly but gently asked him to forgive me . Finally, he melted into my arms and, with tears flowing uncontrollably, he said "Yes, I forgive you, DAD."

Then I said, "Let me speak for your Heavenly Father." I spoke to him saying what I believed God would say to him at that moment. "I created you in My image. I love you. I have always been with you. I will never take My eye off you. I heard your heart cry at night from your bed. I am proud of you. You are My son in whom I am well pleased. I will never turn My back on you. I have redeemed you. You are My precious son." I paused again, then I asked, "Can you trust Me as your Heavenly Father?" He replied softly, "Yes, I can." He clung to me and soaked my shoulder with tears. His weeping turned to sobbing which turned to a healthy emotional total release—blubbering! All I can tell you is that, in that moment, this young man's life was forever changed through a supernatural intervention. The chains fell off his mind and heart, and he was forever free!

The following chapters will provide you with an explanation of the father wound and the way to healing through the Father's Blessing. I will provide examples throughout of those who have experienced healing so that you can see the benefits of this blessing on our life. I hope that this book will give you useful advice on overcoming the challenges that stem from a broken relationship with your earthly father. My prayer is that you can heal that relationship and in doing so, see who your Heavenly Father is, and has always been, in your life.

Your future awaits.

Chapter One

MY EPIPHANY ABOUT

THE FATHER'S BLESSING

My understanding of the need and the power of the Father's
Blessing began with a trip to Toronto, Canada in January 2001.
This encounter changed both my wife, Rivers, and my life forever.
With God, there are no coincidences. Someone once said, "Coincidence is God's way of remaining anonymous." What started
out as a novel idea to deepen our understanding of God launched
us both on a healing path for the restoration of the father wound
through the giving of the Father's Blessing.

As a little background on the genesis of the trip, a woman
in our church offered me $5,000 to take as many congregants as
possible to a conference in Toronto, Canada that she had heard
about. It was a weekend that she thought might encourage anyone who attended, including myself. It was billed as the "Father's
Heart Conference." I asked Rivers if she wanted to attend since
she struggled with the issue of "father" in her own life throughout
our entire marriage. She later shared that something drew her
in when she heard the "heart" part of the conference title, so she
agreed to go. Unbeknownst to me, Rivers had also been struggling
with God issues for a long while. How that escaped my knowledge and attention as her husband, friend, and pastoral covering

of twenty-three years has given me great pause for reflection over time. Personally, I should have been more tuned in to her, but was not. I later learned in her tearful communication that she had been asking God for agonizing months: "Do you really love me? Do you want me? Are you even real?" During this dialogue with God, Rivers asked for a sign to confirm His love. If God would use her name, Rivers, in a sign, then it would be private and personal and no one would ever know the extraordinary dilemma she faced—that of losing her faith, her hope, and maybe even her marriage. This was serious stuff!

We loaded the church van with five lay leaders from the church and left for Toronto a day early due to a pending blizzard forecast to move into the Northeast. As we departed Connecticut, a thick blanket of snow began to fall. So much for the weather forecast! By the time we reached the New York border, heavy blizzard conditions blurred the highway passage and made the road trip even more arduous. We voted to keep going but, about midnight, we were drained by slow progress and decided to find food and gas at the next exit. We made a random right turn and headed down a dark, snow-covered road in search of an open restaurant. After driving a couple of miles with no luck, we decided to head the other direction.

This is the riveting story of how God showed up in a most miraculous way for Rivers, and my hope is that you will understand that God spares no detail to get our attention when the timing is right. Her story begins at the U-turn. Later, Rivers would share:

> As we made the U-turn, I looked out of the icy window and saw a little wooden shack on the side of the

road that was closed for the night. The sign along the eaves of the roof read, "Angel's Restaurant Fried Chicken." Fried chicken happened to be my most favorite Texas food growing up. Angel's Restaurant? Fried Chicken in upstate New York? However, what caught my eye in the seventeen-inch snowstorm was the large, white marquee sign with multiple yellow blinking lights illuminating the falling snow in the front yard of the little wooden restaurant. There were two words on that sign that stunned me: RIVERS WANTED. I absolutely could not believe my eyes. I looked again as the van slowly made its way down the snow-laden road to find food, just to make sure it was as I thought. I had asked God for a sign with my name and here it was on an actual sign. Unbelievable! God had given me a real, honest-to-goodness sign using my own name as asked. But He also gave me something as profound as Rivers on that white board. He said WANTED. He wanted me! Remember my three questions? Are you for real? Do you love me? Do you want me?

I later realized I had never thought about my own name, "Rivers," in the word "Drivers." The "D" had fallen off the sign somewhere in the snow, which was supposed to advertise, "Drivers Wanted." Really! Whatever had happened to that letter D just did not matter. The sign, "Rivers Wanted," did. It was the game changer for my hope. At that moment, my life was turned upside down. I have often reflected on how funny God is. He can have such a hilarious sense of humor when He pops into a life for good. He's a genius! This one massive, miraculous act of God (an actual sign!) changed my life forever. It could not have been more divinely planned and executed.

After twenty or so grueling hours on the road, we arrived at the Toronto church to attend the Father's Heart Conference. It was a two-day conference with various speakers and topics geared to issues of family, crisis management, and the Father's love we all so genuinely need to know in order to survive. We could all identify with the subject matter that each speaker tackled. There was a soaking prayer room Rivers found on the weekend agenda that piqued her interest as a college music major. One could just lie on a pillow and meditate quietly to the beautiful strains of a harp or violin. She found this exercise to be a little out of the box to participate in, but extremely soothing nonetheless. She later shared that she could do nothing but worship God on her back with her eyes closed; emotionally and spiritually losing herself in the fact that God, her Heavenly Father, had genuinely wanted her, as the sign had read. She was able to embrace for the first time the hope birthed through her encounter with God and receive personal ministry to her heart, after so many years of doubt, worry, unease, and fear. A transformational breakthrough.

My First Introduction to the Father's Blessing

During one of the subsequent evening sessions, a guest speaker, Pastor Jack Winter, asked for pastors and their wives to come to the front if they would like prayer. In all the years of ministry we had participated in, no one had ever prayed for us as a couple. An absolute travesty to realize we had not been blessed as a couple, but how many in ministry had really ever had this? I propose, not many after ordination. We ran down the aisle from the back of the auditorium in sheer desperation to meet Pastor Winter, and we were the first in line to ask for that special prayer. His attention was directed towards me first. He came over, and I introduced myself as a Lutheran minister as I asked him for prayer. The first question he asked took me a little off-guard. He wanted to know what type of relationship I had had with my earthly father. "Great, he was an awesome dad" was my reply. Rivers concurred whole-heartedly that Raymond Teske was an awesome dad. He then quietly turned to Rivers and asked the same. All she could do was weep uncontrollably. While Rivers was trying to regain her composure, I shared that she had come from a home where her birth father had left when she was five, and her stepfather had been emotionally absent from nine years of age onward. I listened attentively as he said very lovingly, he was going to give her an earthly father's blessing by standing in as a proxy for her two earthly fathers. She later confessed that she was quite sure four thousand people must have heard the wails coming from the pit of her stomach as he prayed over her. Rivers had to come to terms with the fact that both her fathers had broken her heart and that she needed healing from her deeply wounding "father" relationships of abandonment and lack of any affirmation.

Pastor Winter asked Rivers if he could stand in proxy for her fathers and asked her to forgive them both and release them to God. After a few minutes of substantial resistance and through a veil of tears, she forgave them both and released them to God. It was beautiful to watch.

Admittedly, the most poignant touch was going to be from the Heavenly Father, which Winter administered a few minutes later. It was the "trust" part in Rivers' personal relationship to God that needed to be deeply healed in order for her to reconcile with her Heavenly Father. Winter asked her if she could trust God. Rivers later said that this was about the most loaded and heart-rending question she had to address in her life. After an extremely emotional time with Winter in prayer, she finally said that she could trust God. I was so touched myself to watch my wife as he declared the powerful Father's Blessing over her. The great sign of being wanted on our trip to the conference and then the release of the pain and years of sorrow changed her life and our marriage. As I reflected upon this powerful outpouring, I was also brought back to scripture.

Throughout the Old Testament, Jewish fathers blessed their children. An excellent example of this is found in Genesis 49 where Jacob blesses his twelve sons and prophesies over each of them. Genesis 49:28, "All these are the twelve tribes of Israel, and this is what their father said to them when he blessed them, giving each the blessing appropriate to them." This initiated an ongoing practice where fathers blessed and released their children into life. When and where was the blessing of the father lost in our human family? Why did the Protestants and Catholics sadly not cherish this tradition and rite of passage? It was certainly lost in my Lutheran tradition.

Furthermore, I genuinely believe The Father's Blessing is the single most critical act of love a father can do for his sons and daughters. I believe that a father failing to bless his children with words of affirmation and overt acts of love sets up a potential foundational problem in how people view God. You see, the earthly father is the conduit, lens, or filter through which one sees the Heavenly Father. As your earthly father is, so the Heavenly Father must be. Let me unpack this statement. If your earthly father never affirmed you, blessed you, said he loved you or was proud of you, then you will probably assume that the Heavenly Father is no different and is not going to bless, affirm, love, or be there for you either. If your earthly father was absent or uncaring or abusive, then you will perceive that the Heavenly Father must be absent, uncaring, or abusive. This is the genesis of the father wound, which becomes deeply embedded in the hearts and minds of men and women for life.

These were the deeply-walled issues in Rivers' heart that ultimately had to be addressed and healed: physical and emotional abandonment, trust, feeling unwanted and unloved, inadequacy and, at the core, shame. Hence, the request for the sign she needed from God. "Was she wanted?" Your list may differ. It might include abuse, absenteeism, abandonment, addictions, indifference, controlling, violence, bullying, even the early death of the father, etc. Of course, we all have issues because we are all human and humans fail. If you have had a fabulous relationship with your father, then I celebrate that with you. However, in our ministry experience, most individuals in the world have missed a large chunk of unconditional love because they only know what they know. If your father was less than stellar, then you need a spiritual realignment in your heart, mind, and life. The final piece in this quilt of God can be sewn into place by your Heavenly Father's very own hands. The piece of the quilt is labeled: DIVINE LOVE. This love is almost incomprehensible to understand as a human being. Ultimately, we all have this desire in common: to be loved and to be wanted.

My goal through this book is to give you the absolute reassurance that God the Father accepts you through His Son Jesus Christ, unconditionally. You need to know that He knows and loves you. This blessed assurance will give you total peace knowing that, within the safety net of God's love, you can trust Him to help you forge ahead in this crazy new spiritual life, walking ahead without looking back. This will be uncharted territory, but God's grace will be sufficient for you now and forever.

When I witnessed this great man of God, Pastor Winter, standing in proxy for Rivers' fathers and saw the instantaneous release she received when she forgave them both, subsequently then blessing her as a Daughter Princess of King God, I knew then and there that this was the real deal! The hardest journey was ahead of us in learning to apply the trust that had been addressed. We would have to have the confidence that God knew exactly what He was doing in our life, marriage, and spiritual journey. He was a good God and would carry us along even in the rougher waters when they were to come. This was not the end. This was only the first step.

My introduction into the Ministry of The Father's Blessing to those suffering with a father wound was initiated by Pastor Winter immediately following my wife's impartation of the blessing. Winter turned to me again and asked me about my relationship with my father. I told him that my father was affirming, loving, hugging, and verbally supportive. He had also been a good, solid, Christian man who sowed the foundational tenets of the faith deeply into the hearts of his children. He continued to probe by asking a series of questions about my family life, mother, siblings, etc. After he had exhausted his inquiry, he paused for a few moments. His next words flabbergasted me. He said, "I am going to give you the gift of the impartation of the Father's Blessing for you to give away." I am sure that I had that deer-in-the-headlights stare as he paused. He then wrapped his arms around me in a bear hug and prayed that God would impart the supernatural gift of the impartation of the Father's Blessing upon me.

After the service, we then talked for the next few hours as he mentored me on how to impart the gift. He basically unwrapped the step-by-step process he led Rivers through to restoration and healing. First, he explained the critical reason to speak for the earthly father; ultimately obtaining forgiveness of the father from the one being ministered to. Very simply, the broken heart caused by the father wound has to first be cleared of resentment, disappointment, hurts, bitterness, unforgiveness, and any other residual sins connected to the father to gain healing to clear the pathway to the Heavenly Father. This then opens up the way to establish the ability to trust God. Having a person recognize and honestly embrace trust in their Heavenly Father is the final and most critical step in receiving the blessing. Winter then gave me a bear hug for a second time and prayed that I receive the impartation of the Father's Blessing as a mantle to give away. He held me tightly for a few moments and let me go. I did not feel physical signs, but I remember feeling an incredible peace coupled with a sense of awe and wonderment. I returned to my seat to reflect on all that had transpired for Rivers and me.

My First Impartation of the Father's Blessing

I returned to Connecticut. A few days later, I was speaking to Tim, a man about my age that I had recently met at a men's gathering. In the course of our dialogue, I asked him about his father. He said his father was a hard-working scientist who was emotionally detached from his family. He never affirmed his spouse nor his children, verbally or physically. My friend had attended five universities, but never graduated. He became a banker in one of New York's most prestigious banks and made millions of dollars in his lifetime. During all of his success, he shared that he had never received his father's approval. He ultimately turned to alcohol to sedate the emotional pain he suffered from an emotionally absent father. He was truly a broken man. He eventually lost his job and amassed fortune, which initially led him into a long period of alcohol addiction; however, he found sobriety later in life.

I asked him if he wanted me to pray for him so that God would heal his broken heart. He eagerly said that he wanted this. I walked him through the steps and restoration with his father and Heavenly Father. I then embraced him and imparted the Father's Blessing. He instantaneously broke into sobbing and clung to me fearlessly. He said that it felt like a huge weight had lifted off his soul. From that moment forward, he was completely restored and lived a life of joy and peace. This encounter was as much for me as it was for him! I needed to see firsthand the power of God to restore a person by filling them with His love. After this extraordinary encounter, my focus clearly shifted in healing to include those suffering with the father wound by giving spiritual, emotional, and physical relief of lost years through the impartation of the Father's Blessing. It has been the most humbling and rewarding gift that God has personally entrusted me with in the lost time of despair, health loss, and family disengagement.

I have prayed for countless people, both male and female, to address the father wound and then receive the Father's Blessing. The vast majority have been healed and liberated from this invisible wound of the heart. Do not despair. Hope is just around the corner.

Chapter Two

WHAT IS THE FATHER WOUND?

After years of pastoral care and oversight, I have concluded that every child covets their father's blessing. They deeply desire to know that their father loves them, cares for them, accepts them, is proud of them, and blesses them. They want to hear affirmation from his lips, feel his touch with hugs, know with absolute certainty in their heart that their father unconditionally accepts them, and that they can trust their father. Furthermore, every man and woman needs the sanction of the Father's Blessing spoken over them to release them into life.

When the child's father fails to deliver the emotional affirmation partially or in full, the father wound is embedded into the heart of the child. This wound is hidden deep in the heart but exposed throughout life in a variety of ways.

A child must experience a safe home. Parents always demonstrate what a home is, for good or bad. Fathers too often are absent or negligent in taking responsibility for their family. If a father does not provide a loving, caring, protecting, supportive environment, the family, especially the children, will struggle socially, emotionally, spiritually, and physically. Without a father's blessing, the child is vulnerable to a litany of dysfunctional behaviors—they will become strivers, have insecurities, become promiscuous, deal with abandonment and mental issues, will appear lost, imbalanced, have relationship issues, marital issues, identity problems, feel empty, never attain goals, live a life of sadness, depression, they most likely will deal with addictions to kill the pain, etc.

Children who feel unloved and unwanted will seek affirmation. They can become susceptible to pimps, dominant relationships, failure in school, involvement with drugs or pornography; and many will be exploited by the unthinkable. The net result can be sex-trafficking, prostitution, strip joints, and prison. The consequence of poor parenting is never good. Children, boys, and girls, look to the father for approval and blessing. Void of this, the child is set up for a lifetime of heartache and struggle. In my estimation, most men and women come from father relationships lacking some measure of love, affirmation, and blessing; therefore, it is left up to the children's imagination to observe and come to their own conclusion about what constitutes genuine love for them.

A few years ago, Rivers and I ministered to a woman in Canada who shared her tale of parental woe with us. Her father had left the family when she was five years old. Her mother told her that she only married her father because he got her pregnant. She cruelly told the daughter that her misery stemmed from the pregnancy, and that she would never have married the jerk if it were not for this one element to the relationship. After years of verbal abuse, the daughter moved out of the house at fifteen. She became prey to the street, and her life quickly strayed into drugs, pimps, and prostitution. She had absolutely no self-esteem. She sadly lived to exist. You can imagine the negative thought process and the negative self-worth that she felt. Now in midlife, she is unhappily married and has no children. She is understandably hardened against life and untrusting of all people.

I prayed for her to receive the Father's Blessing which she thoroughly received. She is leaning toward restorative love, though not yet there. We stay in touch and continue to pray for her believing that by God's grace, she can one day receive the fullness of His blessing.

Why do fathers fail in many cases to affirm and bless their children? Primarily because they are products of their own environment. Fathers often grew up never being affirmed or blessed by their fathers. As a result, fathers can only deliver what they know. The Bible addresses this unbroken chain of dysfunctional fathering in the Old Testament.

> *Numbers 14:18, "The Lord is slow to anger, abounding in love and forgiving sin and rebellion. Yet he does not leave the guilty unpunished; he punishes the children for the sin (iniquity) of the parents to the third and fourth generation."*

The word "sin" sometimes translated "iniquity" comes from the Hebrew word AWON which literally means "twisted behavior" or "perverseness." The text is not talking about sin in a generic sense, but specific sinfulness. This implies that whatever perverseness or twisted behavior of the father will be demonstrated through his actions and passed down generationally from father to child.

A Biblical example is found in the Book of Genesis. The great patriarchs of the faith: Abraham, Isaac, and Jacob were human and demonstrated the sinful behavior of lying which was passed down generationally. Abraham, motivated by fear, lied to King Pharaoh about Sarah being his sister and not his wife (Genesis 12). Years later, Isaac, when confronted by King Abimelech, driven by fear also lied to protect himself (Genesis 26). The third-generation offspring, Jacob, lied and fled in fear from his brother, Esau, for his deception. A generation later, Jacob's ten sons lied to their father about the death of their brother, Joseph, whom they despised (Genesis 37). The family legacy of lying was manifested in four generations until it was broken by Joseph. He was an honest man with great integrity, and his trust in God enabled him to overcome lying when faced with uncertainty. When faced with fear, he told the truth regardless of the consequences (Genesis 37-50).

If a child grows up in a home where the father is absent, then abandonment will be the lesson learned by the child. A father can be physically absent due to work, hobbies, friends, divorce, or even death. He can also be emotionally absent because of personality issues or addictive behavior. Whatever the circumstance, the child is more than likely set up for a lifetime of abandonment issues which result in feelings of insecurity, inadequacy, worthlessness and shame, to mention a few.

This is the story of a parishioner named John. He sat in my office, with the appearance of a beaten down, ragged man. He struggled with spending time with his family. He and his wife constantly argued about the amount of time he "put in," as she called it, either at home with his family or in the family's extra-curricular activities. He said that he did not really enjoy spending time with the family even though he knew he should. He was extremely frustrated with his wife and obviously with life. He said they had everything they needed, and he was confused as to why she was unhappy with him. I explored his history as a child, and he told me that his father would leave early for work in the morning and come home late in the evening. His ritual was to pick up his dinner plate, isolate himself in his home office to eat and watch television and go to bed. The mother never interrupted him and strictly enforced the family rule. He was disengaged. The father existed virtually apart from his family while at home. I asked him how he felt about this. He said he lived with anxiety and fear of his father. He found it difficult to speak with his father. He felt that his father loved him because he took care of the family, but he said his father never told him that he loved him. I asked him if he could see a pattern in his life similar to his father's behavior. Amazingly, he initially pushed back from that thought, but eventually gave himself permission to accept the comparison. Once he admitted the parallel between his father and himself, he became open to receive the father's blessing. Once he received the blessing, his life changed. He constantly tells his children that he loves them. He sat down with each one and asked for their forgiveness for anything that he did to hurt them. Furthermore, he verbally blessed each one as his beloved son or daughter. His wife later came to me and expressed her gratitude for my guidance in helping her husband become the loving husband and father she longed for. He spent more time with his family and began to become more verbally expressive of his positive feelings toward them. It was hard work, but he came to acknowledge how he felt about his own father's failures and see how it shaped him in his fathering.

You see, a child can grow up in a home where the father does not express verbal or physical affirmation—hugs, nurture, love, and an invisible emotional wall develops between the father and child. In this, the child is left to draw his own emotional conclusions about fathering. If he never says he loves me, then does he love me? Does he even want me or care about me? Thus, the child is led down a lifelong path of uncertainty about the love of the father.

What is the natural result? Whatever a child experiences at home will shape the way they parent as an adult. If the father was preoccupied with work, hobbies, friends, etc., then this sets the stage for the next generation. If a father demonstrates: abuse, aloofness, isolation, alcoholism, anger, absenteeism, addictions, apathy, the next generation will inherit the twisted behavior or perversity (i.e., AWON) and continue to pass it on generationally unless it is broken.

Awareness of the root of the father wound is essential in moving away from generational dysfunction by breaking the chain of sin. Have you ever done something that was perhaps done to you by your father, and you said, "I just said or did what I said I would never do!" If you can relate to this, then change—stop, turn around and move in a healthy new direction. It is hard to change old habits, but if you sense that this is a necessary shift for your behavior, then it is imperative that you work at making the change.

If you feel the pain of the father wound in your own heart, then I want to encourage you. Healing of the father wound is on the way. The antidote to the father wound is the Father's Blessing – both from your earthly father and your Heavenly Father.

A Broken Heart Healed

A professional woman came to me at a healing service asking me to pray for her allergies. God gave me a word of knowledge for her. I simply asked her "who broke your heart?" She started sobbing and told me that her father had deeply hurt her. He had been verbally abusive to her for her entire life which had left her scarred emotionally and mentally. His cruel and callous behavior left her feeling inadequate, unattractive, and vulnerable to most relationships. She had no self-esteem or self-worth. She had concluded that she was basically worthless and unwanted by anyone. Her immune system had broken down. She was overwhelmed with allergies. No wonder!

We talked through the heartbreak and what had transpired between them. After a long, intense struggle, she ultimately prayed and forgave her father for his abusiveness and gave him to the Lord. Following this cleansing release, I led her down a spiritual pathway for healing which allowed her to receive a blessing from her earthly father through me as her surrogate dad. After this, she was able to see her Heavenly Father as one she could trust with her life. I told her that I believed God would heal her from her allergies as a confirmation of her emotional, spiritual, and physical restoration. She confirmed to me that she was completely healed from her allergies and shares her testimony on a regular basis. In her own words, God healed her father wound and blessed her with health and wholeness beyond her imagination.

If there is anything that you have read thus far that is resonating in your spirit, then stop and reflect. If you are sensing a generational perverseness that has been handed down to you in your family line, then declare it null and void. Here is an exercise for you to begin your personal journey of restoration and life change for you and your family.

Reflection Time

Prayerfully seek the Lord in prayer and ask Him to help you recognize unhealthy behaviors in your life that warrant a full change. Write them down. Then take each item separately before the Lord in prayer and:

1. *Confess:* Admit the unhealthy behavior and declare it no longer be acceptable to you. 1 John 1:9, "If we confess our sins, he is faithful and just and will forgive us our sins and purify us from all unrighteousness."

2. *Repent*: Make a sincere acknowledgement to change your behavior and ask the Lord to give you strength to do so by the Holy Spirit. Acts 3:19, "Repent, then, and turn to God, so that your sins may be wiped out, that times of refreshing may come from the Lord."

3. *Change*: Completely change your behavior. Romans 12:1-2, "Therefore I urge you, brethren, by the mercies of God, to present your bodies a living and holy sacrifice, acceptable to God, which is your spiritual service of worship. And do not be conformed to this world, but be transformed by the renewing of your mind, so that you may prove what the will of God is, that which is good and acceptable and perfect."

4. *Commit*: Stick to it! Proverbs 16:3, "Commit to the LORD whatever you do, and he will establish your plans."

These steps brought to completion will prepare you for what is yet to come.

Chapter Three

THE FATHER'S BLESSING

The Missing Pieces

Have you ever put a 1000-piece jigsaw puzzle together only to find that there was a missing piece? You frantically search to find that one missing piece. No luck! Then you try to convince yourself that the "one missing piece of the jigsaw puzzle" does not actually matter. You do not need it to accept the victory of the conquest to complete the puzzle. Yet, as you strain to mentally ascend to that level of acceptance, your eyes remain focused on the empty spot where the lost piece of the 1000-piece Jigsaw puzzle is MISSING! We all understand incompleteness. It is like playing baseball with eight players or playing in a golf tournament with seventeen holes. It just will not work.

There are two areas of importance in every person's life that must be completed. One is in the natural realm; the other is in the spiritual realm. In the natural, every human being desires to know that their earthly father loves him and blesses him unconditionally. Secondly, the father's blessing is a crucial step enabling one to accept the love and blessing in the spiritual realm from the Heavenly Father. Over years of personally ministering to people with a father wound, I have concluded through prayer and observation that the earthly father is the filter through whom a person perceives the Heavenly Father.

I believe, deep down, that within every person is the need to know with absolute certainty that his earthly father loves him. That he is proud of him. A man or woman without this confirmation of the father's total approval will be wanting in his or her soul. He will never feel complete, confident, or capable of being loved without the father's affirmation and blessing. In my pastoral experience, this is the missing piece of the puzzle.

I strongly believe that knowing the father's love and receiving the father's blessing releases a person into manhood or womanhood. Furthermore, the father's love coupled to the father's blessing launches one into life with confidence and assurance. Fathers must clearly communicate verbally by telling their children that they love them and bless them. These are two crucial pieces of life which completes a child's self-image and opens the child up to receive the love and blessing of his Heavenly Father in the spiritual realm.

Within every person, there exists a hole in the soul that only God can fill. The one missing piece—a God-shaped hole that only God can complete. St. Augustine said it this way, "Thou hast created us for Thyself, and our heart is not quiet until it rests in Thee."

Everyone needs to know and hear that God loves him and that He blesses him and that he can trust Him. His Word declares this in so many places.

> Romans 5:5, "And hope does not put us to shame, because God's love has been poured out into our hearts through the Holy Spirit, who has been given

to us."

*1 John 4:7-12, "Dear friends, let us love one anoth-
er, for love comes from God. Everyone who loves
has been born of God and knows God. Whoever
does not love does not know God, because God is
love. This is how God showed his love among us:
He sent his one and only Son into the world that
we might live through him. This is love: not that we
loved God, but that he loved us and sent his Son as
an atoning sacrifice for our sins. Dear friends, since
God so loved us, we also ought to love one another.
No one has ever seen God; but if we love one another, God lives in us and his love is made complete in
us."*

God's Blessing Matters

In Genesis, God sees that everything He created was good and
He blessed it. (Genesis 1:22; 28). The word in Hebrew for "blessed" is barach (bah-rahch) (Strongs #1288) which means "to bless,
salute, congratulate, thank, praise, to kneel down." God spoke to
His newly created family, Adam, and Eve, to bless them with the
capacity to live a full life.

Our first parents, Adam and Eve are a Biblical example (Genesis 1-3) of receiving the blessing of God and losing it not only for
themselves, but for all humanity to follow.

Adam and Eve received the fullness of God's blessing—a
perfect life in paradise. They were sinless, walked and talked with

God, and charged with the caretaking of God's earth. We can only imagine what this must have been like. Additionally, God gave them three mandates:

1. Permission: you can eat of any tree in the Garden of Eden

2. Prohibition: do not eat of the Tree of Knowledge

3. Purpose: tend the garden and have children

Why these three mandates? First, permission gave freedom to life with the opportunity to make good choices with healthy pursuits. Secondly, prohibition provided guidelines, boundaries, structure, and order. Adam and Eve were told not to eat of the Tree of Knowledge of Good and Evil "lest they die." By obeying God, they demonstrated their love and respect for Him as the object of their affection. Thirdly, purpose provided a reason for life with a measured amount of responsibility to "care for the garden." These are like the three legs on a stool. All three—permission, prohibition, and purpose—are necessary to allow the stool to function properly. If you remove one of the legs, the stool obviously topples over. The structure is broken. All Adam and Eve had to do was to demonstrate their love for God by simply obeying the three divine mandates. Their life was peaceful, joyful, and easy. They had no lack.

What happened? They blew it! (Genesis 3). What was the anatomy of the fall from God's grace? Satan came into the garden and began a dialogue with Adam and Eve. Once he had their attention, he planted a seed of doubt in their mind by challenging the truth of God's Word. He asked them if God really meant what

He said and, as soon as Adam and Eve questioned in their mind the veracity of His Word, they were on their way out. The next step was to act on what they questioned. They rebelled. They took the bite! You know the story—it was finished.

The writer of Psalm 1 gives us a warning when he writes about spending time with the ungodly. Psalm 1:1, "Blessed is the one who does not walk in step with the wicked or stand in the way that sinners take or sit in the company of mockers…"

The psalmist gives us a three-legged stool that leads to distraction. Walking can lead to standing which leads to sitting and then, "It is finished!" The way out is the same as it would have been for Adam and Eve, if something or someone challenges the Word of God, flee! Take the advice of God's Word and run the other way.

James 4:7, "Submit yourselves then to God. Resist the devil and he will flee." Because of the drastic result of Adam and Eve's rebellion; sin, death and damnation entered the world and has been passed on to all humanity. As the Bible says:

Romans 5:12, "Therefore, just as sin entered the world through one man, and death through sin, and in this way, death came to all people, because all sinned."

This means that the sin of Adam and Eve was not only embedded into us as sinful nature, but, like them, it separated us from our Heavenly Father. They were banished forever from the Garden of Eden.

God declared that mankind could be restored to Him as their Heavenly Father through these words known as the first Gospel proclamation. Genesis 3:15, "And I will put enmity between you and the woman, and between your offspring and hers; he will crush your head, and you will strike his heel."

God is prophetically speaking about the coming of His Son, Jesus Christ, who will be born from a human woman. Satan will attempt to disrupt God the Father's plan of salvation, but will be destroyed by the blood of the Lamb on the cross. His son Jesus then is the sacrifice, which enables all humanity the opportunity to be restored to their Heavenly Father.

Adam and Eve each received a curse tailored to their gender as a man and woman.

Adam's Curse

Genesis 3:17-19, "To Adam he said, 'Because you listened to your wife and ate fruit from the tree about which I commanded you, 'You must not eat from it,' 'the ground because of you; through painful toil you will eat food from it all the days of your life. It will produce thorns and thistles for you, and you will eat the plants of the field. By the sweat of your brow, you will eat your food until you return to the ground, since from it you were taken; for dust you are and to dust you will return.'"

Adam's curse meant he was going to have to "earn a living" by the sweat of his brow in the face of challenges. Another way of saying it is, "There is no free lunch!" He was going to have to strive to exist.

Of course, the logical spin-off of this curse was the need for man to develop a career. To succeed in a career, one must be driven, focused, and uncompromising. Success is finding approval, affirmation, and acceptance from one's boss no matter the cost. Career supersedes everything else. The picture is this: man left the garden to inherit the curse of chasing his career.

Eve's Curse

Genesis 3:16, "To the woman he said, 'I will make your pains in childbearing very severe; with painful labor you will give birth to children. Your desire will be for your husband, and he will rule over you.'"

Eve received two curses from God. The first is the obvious one that every person (especially women) can understand: "pain in childbearing will be severe." I was there for the birth of my three children, and I can attest to the fact that it appears to be extremely arduous. My only connection to the pain of childbirth is that I have passed several kidney stones which I hear can be excruciatingly similar. Ouch!

The second curse spoken to the woman is: "your desire will be for your husband, and he will rule over you." How does this translate? There no longer exists a mutuality of purpose and support in a bilateral way, but a tandem effort of the man chasing his career and the woman chasing her husband whom she desires. The man has taken the lead and the woman is playing second fiddle to his career. Before "sin" entered the world, everything was in perfect order, harmony, and balance. After sin entered the scene, disruption, confusion, and chaos dominated the once healthy relationship between man and woman.

In this broken state of relationship, if the woman cannot catch the man she desires, she will become the man she cannot catch. This conclusion may sound offensive, but it can be accurately substantiated in our society today. A woman needs affirmation, acceptance, and approval. If she cannot get it from the man she desires, she will find validation one way or another. I am reminded of a song Marc Almond made famous, "Looking for love in all the wrong places."

Before sin destroyed the relationship between God and man, they were basking in the Father's Blessing. Even though it was lost through a horrible choice, the need for that blessing is still longed for in the soul of every person. I genuinely believe that every man and woman desires to receive his or her father's blessing; children long to know that their father loves them; that he is proud of them. This blessing must come from the earthly father as well as from the Heavenly Father.

If a man does not receive his father's blessing, he too often becomes a striver. He will set arbitrary goals that he believes will garner his father's respect but, once he reaches that goal, it will not bring satisfaction. He will keep moving the bar higher and higher while never finding acceptance. Over my forty-five plus years of ministry, I have known several men who have gained great wealth, filtered through marriages and affairs, collected homes and assorted trophies, and continued to keep the throttle down as they worked even though they did not need a single material thing. Why? They never received their father's blessing. Possessions, power, and position cannot replace a father's blessing which includes love, affirmation, and acceptance!

If a woman does not know that her father loves her (which I believe she needs to hear repeatedly) and does not have his blessing, she will become vulnerable to not feeling good enough, smart enough, pretty enough. She will develop low self-esteem, low self-image, no self-worth, and no respect. She will believe she is worthless. She will feel like a throwaway. Many times, from observation, I have noted that a woman who has never received her father's blessing may become a man-pleaser. She can become sexually active seeking love or allow an abusive relationship to overtake her life.

Sadly, men and women will seek pacification of their pain in the empty hole of their soul from not having the father's blessing through food, sex, drugs, alcohol, work, tobacco, etc.

As I reflect on writing this book, I could share hundreds of stories that come to mind of men and women who have lived out painful emotional lives because they have never received their father's blessing. The quest for the father's blessing is the theme in many books, television sitcoms and movies. Why? Because it is such a familiar narrative that most understand.

When a father is negligent and fails to love, protect, and provide a covering for his wife and children, God will take the lead. These Bible passages speak to God's heart for the defenseless:

James 1:27, "Religion that God our Father accepts as pure and faultless is this: to look after orphans and widows in their distress..."

Psalm 68:5, "A father to the fatherless, a defender of widows, is God in his holy dwelling."

Job 29:12, "I rescued the poor who cried for help, and the fatherless who had none to assist them."

I believe this also includes the single mothers and their babies in our 21st Century culture—these are the "widows and orphans" of our times.

The responsibility to love, provide and protect the family— wife and children—belongs to the father. When the father reneges on his responsibilities, family problems arise, and the family is fractured. Hence, our broken society.

What is the antidote to the curse?

Throughout the Old Testament, a person would kneel to speak or receive a blessing from either God, the king, or a father to launch them into their manhood. Abraham, Isaac, and Jacob all blessed their sons with a father's blessing to release them into the world.

Do you realize that Jesus did not begin His ministry until He received His Father's blessing? Jesus was raised by Mary and Joseph in Nazareth in Galilee. Although Joseph was His earthly father, he was not His biological father (Luke 1). When Jesus was thirty years old (Luke 3:23), He began His ministry; but He did not commence until He received His Heavenly Father's blessing.

He made His way to the Jordan River where He was baptized by His cousin, John the Baptist. At that moment, a voice from Heaven declared: "This is My Son, whom I love; with Him I am well pleased" (Luke 3:22). This was the Heavenly Father's blessing which came directly from the mouth of God Himself. Jesus did not begin his ministry until he received his Father's blessing.

The result of God blessing Jesus and releasing Him into ministry is echoed in the words of the Apostle Peter in Acts 10:38 "How God anointed Jesus of Nazareth with the Holy Spirit and power, and how He went around doing good and healing all who were under the power of the devil, because God was with him."

The Father's Blessing was essential in releasing Jesus into His ministry to fulfill His divine purpose. So, what was the objective for the life of Jesus Christ? To restore broken humanity to the Heavenly Father through the cross and empty tomb. Adam and Eve fell from grace and placed all humanity on a road to perdition. The pathway to paradise breaks the curse for all who believe that

Jesus Christ died on the cross for their sin and rose from the dead to provide the gift of everlasting life. The antidote to the curse is Jesus Christ.

God Designs Families

But we still live in a broken world, marred by sin. As a result, we are wounded—particularly by those closest to us. I believe that the most crucial relationship, the one that sets the stage for all others, is the relationship between the father and oneself. God established the relationship of the earthly father to His child to be a model for the child to understand a healthy connection to the Heavenly Father. When sin entered in, all human relationships were corrupted which was Satan's plan all along. With these foundational relationships damaged, Satan has an easy pathway to distort a healthy understanding of the Heavenly Father. Satan uses our sinful emotional baggage to cloud our view of God. It is only through the redemptive work of the cross that the curse can be broken, and the garbage of life cleaned up. Faith in Jesus Christ is the antidote to the curse.

Galatians 3:13, "Christ redeemed us from the curse of the law by becoming a curse for us, for it is written: "Cursed is everyone who is hung on a pole."

Paul says that, out of reverence for Christ as His followers, we are obligated to submit to one another. Then he shows how believers, filled with the Holy Spirit, can live together in a practical way in a variety of human relationships with mutual love and responsibilities which restore the harmony lost in the Garden of Eden.

The broken world understands the cursed life of Adam and Eve. Only a born-again believer, whose eyes are open, can see how the restored Kingdom of God was meant to be before Adam and Eve sinned. Paul clearly addresses the role of the believers who live a life where the curse is broken and blessed restoration awaits.

> *Ephesians 5:21-6:4, "Submit to one another out of reverence for Christ. Wives submit yourselves to your own husbands as you do to the Lord. For the husband is the head of the wife as Christ is the head of the church, his body, of which he is the Savior. Now as the church submits to Christ, so also wives should submit to their husbands in everything. Husbands, love your wives, just as Christ loved the church and gave Himself up for her to make her holy, cleansing her by the washing with water through the word, and to present her to Himself as a radiant church, without stain or wrinkle or any other blemish, but holy and blameless. In this same way, husbands ought to love their wives as their own bodies. He who loves his wife loves himself. After all, no one ever hated their own body, but they feed and care for their body, just as Christ does the church— for we are members of His body. 'For this reason, a man will leave his father and mother and be united to his wife, and the two will become one flesh.'*

This is a profound mystery—but I am talking about Christ and the church. However, each one of you also must love his wife as he loves himself, and the wife must respect her husband. Children, obey your parents in the Lord, for this is right. 'Honor your father and mother' which is the first commandment with a promise' so that it may go well with you and that you may enjoy long life on the earth.' Fathers do not exasperate your children; instead, bring them up in the training and instruction of the Lord."

Paul says that a husband must love his wife so much that he would be willing to die for her as Christ died for His Bride, the Church. Furthermore, a father must raise his child with Godly training, which also must be exemplified in the father's life.

This includes love, protection, provision, and blessing. If fathers would take this Biblical admonition to heart and live it out daily, families would grow stronger and healthier. Children would mature into loving husbands and wives. Even the nations would be healthier if they would implement this Biblical principle!

Dads:

- Tell your kids you love them and that you are proud of them
- Bless them
- Hug them
- Affirm them
- Encourage them
- Honor your word
- Make promises you can keep
- Set realistic expectations
- Bring them up in the knowledge of the Lord Jesus

Christ

- Teach them to worship the Living God—Father, Son
and Holy Spirit

The way they experience you will determine how they perceive
God.

> *Proverbs 22:6, "Start children off on the way they*
> *should go, and even when they are old, they will not*
> *turn from it."*

Chapter Four

A FAUX BLESSING

A Tale of Two Brothers – Esau and Jacob

The Book of Genesis tells us about twin brothers who entered a lifetime struggle over a fake father's blessing. The complete narrative is recorded in Genesis 25-33, but I want to share a paraphrased version to make my point about the consequences of an illegitimate blessing. This is not to be confused with the "birthright" that Esau sold to his brother, Jacob, for a pot of stew in ancient times. The birthright included the inheritance rights of the firstborn male child which would later be validated by the Father's Blessing.

> *Genesis 25:19-34, "This is the account of the family line of Abraham's son Isaac.*
>
> *Abraham became the father of Isaac, and Isaac was forty years old when he married Rebekah, daughter of Bethuel the Aramean from Paddan Aram and sister of Laban the Aramean. Isaac prayed to the Lord on behalf of his wife because she was childless. The Lord answered his prayer, and his wife Rebekah became pregnant. The babies jostled each other*

within her, and she said, 'Why is this happening to me?' So, she went to inquire of the Lord. The Lord said to her,

'Two nations are in your womb, and two peoples from within you will be separated; one people will be stronger than the other, and the older will serve the younger.' When the time came for her to give birth, there were twin boys in her womb. The first to come out was red, and his whole body was like a hairy garment; so, they named him Esau. After this, his brother came out, with his hand grasping Esau's heel; so, he was named Jacob. Isaac was sixty years old when Rebekah gave birth to them. The boys grew up, and Esau became a skillful hunter, a man of the open country, while Jacob was content to stay at home among the tents. Isaac, who had a taste for wild game, loved Esau, but Rebekah loved Jacob. Once when Jacob was cooking some stew, Esau came in from the open country, famished. He said to Jacob, 'Quick, let me have some of that red stew! I'm famished!' (That is why he was also called Edom.) Jacob replied, 'First sell me your birthright.' 'Look, I am about to die,' Esau said. 'What good is the birthright to me?' But Jacob said, 'Swear to me first.' So, he swore an oath to him, selling his birthright to Jacob. Then Jacob gave Esau some bread and some lentil stew. He ate and drank, and then got up and left. So, Esau despised his birthright."

Isaac and Rebekah had twin sons. Esau was the firstborn by a few seconds and his brother was called Jacob. Esau had red hair and a hairy body. He enjoyed hunting and was his father's favorite. Jacob was mild mannered and closer to his mother. The name Jacob literally means "grasp the heel" (figuratively meaning 'deceives').

Father Isaac was aging and blind and called Esau to prepare a meal for him. Isaac wanted to bless his son with an irrevocable blessing. Esau left to hunt for game. Rebekah sent Jacob in to lie to his father by announcing that he was Esau. Blind Isaac then proceeded to bless Jacob who then made a quick exit. Esau returned and he and his father realized that Jacob had stolen his blessing.

> *Genesis 27:34-41, "When Esau heard his father's words, he burst out with a loud and bitter cry and said to his father, 'Bless me too, my father!' But he said, 'Your brother came deceitfully and took your blessing.' Esau said, 'Isn't he rightly named Jacob? This is the second time he has taken advantage of me: He took my birthright, and now he has taken my blessing!' Then he asked, 'Haven't you reserved any blessing for me?' Isaac answered Esau, 'I have made him lord over you and have made all his relatives his servants, and I have sustained him with grain and new wine. So, what can I possibly do for you, my son?' Esau said to his father, 'Do you have only one blessing, my father? Bless me too, my father!' Then Esau wept aloud...Esau held a grudge against Jacob because of the blessing his father had*

given him. He said to himself, 'The days of mourn-
ing for my father are near; then I will kill my brother
Jacob.'"

Esau tried to separate the birthright from the blessing, but the for-
mer led inevitably to the latter since both involved the inheritance
of the firstborn.

Rebekah told Jacob to flee to his Uncle Laban in Haran. Jacob
left and spent the next twenty years with his uncle, where he pros-
pered greatly. He had two wives, eleven sons, large flocks of sheep,
goats, and a surplus of servants. Despite all his wealth and success,
he had no peace. He had the appearance of living a blessed life, but
he knew that the blessing he had stolen for Esau was illegitimate.

After many prosperous years with his uncle, Jacob finally decided that the time had arrived for him to return home. As he approached the border of his homeland, Jacob sent messengers ahead
to inform Esau of his return. Upon the return of Jacob's men, the
following political maneuvering is worth a review:

Genesis 32:6-21, "When the messengers returned
to Jacob, they said, 'We went to your brother Esau,
and now he is coming to meet you, and four hun-
dred men are with him.' In great fear and distress
Jacob divided the people who were with him into
two groups, and the flocks and herds and camels as
well. He thought, 'If Esau comes and attacks one
group, the group that is left may escape.' Then Jacob
prayed, 'O God of my father Abraham, God of my
father Isaac, Lord, you who said to me, 'Go back

to your country and your relatives, and I will make you prosper,' I am unworthy of all the kindness and faithfulness you have shown your servant. I had only my staff when I crossed this Jordan, but now I have become two camps. Save me, I pray, from the hand of my brother Esau, for I am afraid he will come and attack me, and the mothers with their children. But you have said, 'I will surely make you prosper and will make your descendants like the sand of the sea, which cannot be counted.' He spent the night there, and from what he had with him he selected a gift for his brother Esau: two hundred female goats and twenty male goats, two hundred ewes and twenty rams, thirty female camels with their young, forty cows and ten bulls, and twenty female donkeys and ten male donkeys. He put them in the care of his servants, each herd by itself, and said to his servants, 'Go ahead of me, and keep some space between the herds.' He instructed the one in the lead: 'When my brother Esau meets you and asks, 'Who do you belong to, and where are you going, and who owns all these animals in front of you?' then you are to say, 'They belong to your servant Jacob. They are a gift sent to my lord Esau, and he is coming behind us." He also instructed the second, the third and all the others who followed the herds: 'You are to say the same thing to Esau when you meet him. And be sure to say, 'Your servant Jacob is coming behind us." For he thought, 'I will pacify him with these gifts I

am sending on ahead; later, when I see him, perhaps
he will receive me.' So, Jacob's gifts went on ahead of
him, but he himself spent the night in the camp."

The text implies that Jacob did everything he could to buffer the collision with his potentially hostile brother, Esau. He prayed to God for protection. He positioned most of his earthly possessions across the river to possibly pacify Esau. Why? Because he had deceptively taken what was not rightfully his—the blessing! Ironically, the same fear he left with twenty years earlier still plagued him. That is the nature of unresolved guilt.

Jacob did the best he could do to prepare for the encounter; but he did not count on the real encounter yet to come.

Genesis 32:22-31, "That night Jacob got up and
took his two wives, his two female servants and his
eleven sons and crossed the ford of the Jabbok. After
he had sent them across the stream, he sent over all
his possessions. So, Jacob was left alone, and a man
wrestled with him till daybreak. When the man saw
that he could not overpower him, he touched the
socket of Jacob's hip so that his hip was wrenched as
he wrestled with the man. Then the man said, 'Let
me go, for it is daybreak.' But Jacob replied, 'I will
not let you go unless you bless me.' The man asked
him, 'What is your name?' 'Jacob,' he answered. Then
the man said, 'Your name will no longer be Jacob,
but Israel, because you have struggled with God and
with humans and have overcome.' Jacob said, 'Please

tell me your name.' But he replied, 'Why do you ask my name?' Then he blessed him there. So, Jacob called the place Peniel, saying, 'It is because I saw God face to face, and yet my life was spared.' The sun rose above him as he passed Peniel, and he was limping because of his hip."

What was the benefit for Jacob during and after his struggle with God?

Most importantly, Jacob, now Israel, finally received a real father's blessing! He was finally at peace with God and man. Jacob made an honest attempt to return the 'blessing' to Esau that he had illegitimately received from Isaac, because he knew in his heart that the Father's Blessing he received from God was all he would need for the rest of his life.

> *Genesis 33:11, "Please accept the present (same word in Hebrew for 'blessing') that was brought to you, for God has been gracious to me and I have all I need.' And because Jacob insisted, Esau accepted it."*

Though Esau hesitated initially to take the blessing his father, Isaac, had deceptively given to Jacob, he took it. Esau had lived a lifetime with no father's blessing, and he had the blessing he cried out for twenty years earlier. This enabled the wound in his heart to finally be healed. Regardless of your age or circumstance, it is never too late to receive your father's blessing.

What were the consequences for Jacob? His name was changed to Israel which means 'struggles with God.' When you encounter the Living God face to face, several things will happen:

When you wrestle with God:

- He will always win
- It will cost you something (Jacob limped the rest of his life as a reminder)
- He will change you (name change)
- He will disrupt your paradigm in a good way; both for yourself and for God

Jacob went through a spiritual transformation. He was changed from:

- Striver to satisfied
- Dishonest to honest
- Wheeling and dealing to accepting
- Discontent to content
- Fake to authentic

When you receive the Heavenly Father's blessing, your life will be transformed too.

So, what is stopping you if you have not yet received your natural father's blessing? Furthermore, the way you see your earthly father determines the way you will perceive your heavenly one. If your father was distant: God will appear to be distant. If your earthly father was angry, aloof, absent, abusive, untrustworthy, then why would God be any different than your father? The father wound in your heart is caused by uncertainty of your father's love and is deep. Trust violated by man yields absence of trust in God.

This is the story of Steve. A man in his late sixties who grew up in a home where his father never gave any form of affirmation. His father never hugged him, said "I love you" or "I am proud of you." The man coveted his father's approval. The man played a variety of sports in high school. His favorite sport, which he went on to play in college, was basketball. During his junior year, he was in a pre-game warmup drill when he looked up and saw his father sitting in the stands. His mind was flooded by exuberance, because this was the first sporting event his father had come to see.

The young man played his heart out; and even though his team lost by one point, he scored more points than any previous game. He spotted his father walking down the bleachers and ran to him. He asked him, "What did you think?" His father said, "You lost!" and turned around, walked away and never came to another of his son's sporting events.

These two words spoken by his father set him up for a life-time of striving and trying to prove himself. He set up an artificial benchmark for himself to achieve. The problem was that every time he reached his goal, it never gave him satisfaction. So, he would set another goal that he would achieve only to feel incomplete. So again, and again he would set higher benchmarks to achieve only to feel completely unfulfilled. He lived as a habitual "striver." Though he made millions of dollars, it cost two marriages, relationships with his children and grandchildren, friends, and colleagues. His life was saturated with regrets and a strong sense of unworthiness. He had never had a need for God—or anyone else for that matter—until he met me.

In our initial meeting, he told me that he thought that I was a clergy wimp, but we had a common denominator. We both played golf. We became friends. After a while, I had parity with him and eventually earned his trust. With God's help, I guided him as he walked through his past. Together with the Lord, we were able to face his father wounds and, eventually, he was able to forgive his father and look to his Heavenly Father. He finally let go of the striving and began to trust in God. He no longer let his earthly father be the filter through which he perceived his Heavenly Father. He lives in peace with himself today.

Chapter Five

THE FATHER WOUND DOES NOT DISCRIMINATE

The father wound does not discriminate. It affects male or female, rich or poor, educated or uneducated, clergy or laity, white collar, blue collar, no collar. There is no exemption from this invisible wound. Every race, creed, national origin, or political persuasion is vulnerable to it. I have seen and heard the good, the bad and the ugly over the course of my ordained ministry since 1976. Every story is unique though, sadly enough, too often quite similar. If there is a common denominator in most of the personal narratives, it is the fractured, dysfunctional relationship between a father and his child. The net result is almost always the same: an empty soul in search of the father's blessing.

Many years ago, Rivers and I met a woman through sheer coincidence whom I will call Nancy. Someone had given her Rivers' business card, and she tracked her down to see if she could buy a few jackets for her store in Maine that Rivers had designed and manufactured. Over the next year, we became friends, and she extended an invitation to visit her home and business. It was a late autumn day when we arrived in the small picturesque New England village. Winding our way through the quaint hamlet, we drove down a lane through a large iron gate supported by two tall granite columns. I remember stopping the car as we arrived at the stately 1920s old stone home and thinking how magnificent the landscaping was surrounding the estate facing the Atlantic Ocean. I am not one to get overly dramatic on real estate, but this was a jaw-dropping piece of prime property of twenty or so acres, worthy of a design magazine. Nancy greeted us warmly and led us to her large three-room guest suite on the second floor where we not only had a spectacular view of the ocean but overlooked the manicured gardens. I just remember Rivers and I looking out the small glass-paned windows and simultaneously, exclaiming "WOW!"

We spent the weekend with Nancy, sharing stories and deepening our friendship with one another in front of a massive fireplace in overstuffed leather chairs. She told us that she came from an affluent New England family with Pre-Revolutionary roots and had walked the life pathway from high society debutante in New York to girl's school and college, after which she married into an equally established aristocratic New England family. Though she wanted children, she eventually came to the painful realization that she was hopelessly barren. After several years of marriage and multiple affairs on her husband's part, she decided to divorce him. She said that she contemplated remarrying, but the thought of not being able to have children coupled with the fact that she felt "perfectly happy and independent" without a husband, kept her single. She told us that she had evolved into a forceful competitor in business and had become extremely successful in building a small empire. Over the course of her lifetime, she had set high expectations for herself, which she admitted at times were even too high to accomplish, but good because it motivated her to continue the quest. From her own self-evaluation, she absolutely came across as a ferocious lioness, but she didn't seem so to me. She gave me the impression of being lonely, sad, and completely unfulfilled.

Nancy believed she had a wonderful relationship with her family, though she was raised by au pairs while her socialite mother engaged in many activities and relegated her nurturing care to them. Her father was "an extremely busy man," and absent much of the time but, when he was with her, he challenged her to succeed. He also came from a generation of men who did not verbalize any affection. I dug a little deeper about their relationship and she was quick to say that she knew he loved her, although she could not remember him ever saying the actual words to her. However, she did share a very poignant and thought-provoking narrative about her father that I remember to this day.

When Nancy was about five years old, the family would visit their summer home. Her father would often give her the same task to perform every summer. He would hand her a large, brown paper bag and tell her that if she would fill it to the top with clover and leave it on the front steps of the house, he would reward her efforts with a one dollar bill the next day. Her response of course, was to assault the yard and pull every piece of clover she could find, until the bag was filled to the brim. She would then place it proudly on the porch and wait.

The next morning, her father would pick up the bag and tell her that she had not accomplished the mission. The bag was only half-full. He would then proceed to tell her that she needed to try again and work harder. She said that she filled the bag many times and left it on the porch only to have the same outcome. What was going on? Unfortunately, she did not find out the truth for years. Her father would let the bag sit on the porch overnight and the moisture in the clover would evaporate causing the plucked plants to shrink making the bag half-full. As a result, the trusting little girl was confused, frustrated, and disheartened. Her father never gave her the one-dollar reward. Never.

She said that when she later realized what had happened, she confronted her father. Her father simply dismissed the prank as a training exercise to teach her never to trust anyone. The message was clearly received and adopted. Nancy was destined to live a life devoid of trust. She found that she could not trust any man, and this cascaded over into her perception of God. Though she attended church as a child, God was not one she believed she could trust either.

She grew up as an agnostic at best and never felt a need for God. Rivers and I shared the gospel with her and while she listened, she also debated her reasons for not believing in God. At the end, she was politely non-responsive. I believe that the word of God never goes out and returns empty, but I also knew at the time it was going to take a miraculous intervention on the Holy Spirit's part to bring her into the kingdom. But is that not always the case? We drove back to Connecticut with sadness and heavy hearts. We had a wonderful weekend but felt that we had more to do in trying to help our friend Nancy. We continued to stay connected, but our relationship with her dissipated over a few years because of time and distance. Eventually we lost contact with her.

In hindsight, if I knew then what I know now about the power of the impartation of the Father's Blessing, that weekend many years ago may have turned out much differently. At that time, Rivers and I were limited in our understanding of the real healing power of God which is still active and alive today through Jesus Christ. This was revealed to us later through the empowering of the Holy Spirit in our lives.

Dwelling on what could have been on that beautiful autumn weekend in Maine gives license to conjuring up regrets. The past is behind us. God does not want us to look back at the past.

> *Luke 9:62, "Jesus replied, 'No one who puts a hand to the plow and looks back is fit for service in the kingdom of God.'"*

However, the "present" is only for a moment and is gone in an augenblick—German for "blink of an eye". Therefore, we have learned to carpe diem and seize the day. Opportunities quickly come and quickly go. Furthermore, we believe that we must always live with the future in mind, for that is where we meet our ongoing opportunities to serve God by serving others.

> *Philippians 3:13-16, "Brothers and sisters, I do not consider myself yet to have taken hold of it. But one thing I do: Forgetting what is behind and straining toward what is ahead, I press on toward the goal to win the prize for which God has called me heavenward in Christ Jesus. All of us, then, who are mature should take such a view of things. And if on some point you think differently, that too God will make clear to you. Only let us live up to what we have already attained."*

Chapter Six

JESUS IS THE FATHER WOUND HEALER

But for those who have had a less than perfect paternal relationship, there is hope for restoration through Jesus Christ when you are born again. Jesus Christ came into the world to restore humankind to the Heavenly Father. Please read the following Bible passages with a prayerful, open heart.

> *John 3:3-18, "Jesus replied, 'Very truly I tell you,*
> *no one can see the kingdom of God unless they are*
> *born again.' 'How can someone be born when they*
> *are old?" Nicodemus asked. 'Surely they cannot enter*
> *a second time into their mother's womb to be born!'*
> *Jesus answered, 'Very truly I tell you, no one can*
> *enter the kingdom of God unless they are born of*
> *water and the Spirit. Flesh gives birth to flesh, but*
> *the Spirit gives birth to spirit. You should not be*
> *surprised at my saying, 'You must be born again.' The*
> *wind blows wherever it pleases. You hear its sound,*
> *but you cannot tell where it comes from or where it*
> *is going. So, it is with everyone born of the Spirit.'*
> *'How can this be?' Nicodemus asked. 'You are Israel's*
> *teacher,' said Jesus, 'and do you not understand these*
> *things? Very truly I tell you, we speak of what we*

know, and we testify to what we have seen, but still, you people do not accept our testimony. I have spoken to you of earthly things, and you do not believe; how then will you believe if I speak of heavenly things? No one has ever gone into heaven except the one who came from heaven – the Son of Man. Just as Moses lifted the snake in the wilderness, so the Son of Man must be lifted-up, that everyone who believes may have eternal life in him.' For God so loved the world that he gave his one and only Son, that whoever believes in him shall not perish but have eternal life. For God did not send his Son into the world to condemn the world, but to save the world through him. Whoever believes in him is not condemned, but whoever does not believe stands condemned already because they have not believed in the name of God's one and only Son."

The beauty of this passage is that it gives you a way to restoration with your Heavenly Father. Allow the Spirit of God to illuminate you with the truth about Christ. Why? You must be born again to be restored into that perfect relationship that Adam and Eve enjoyed prior to their—and, ultimately, your—fall from grace. And how do you know you are back in relationship with your Heavenly Father? Verse 3: Jesus replied, "Very truly I tell you, no one can see the kingdom of God unless they are born again."

Do you see the Kingdom of God? If you do, you are in; if you do not, then go back and prayerfully read again asking God to give you a personal epiphany by the Holy Spirit, then you will find great joy in what the great Apostle Paul writes to the Galatian church.

> *Galatians 3:26-4:7, "So in Christ Jesus you are all children of God through faith, for all of you who were baptized into Christ have clothed yourselves with Christ. There is neither Jew nor Gentile, neither slave nor free, nor is there male and female, for you are all one in Christ Jesus. If you belong to Christ, then you are Abraham's seed, and heirs according to the promise. What I am saying is that if an heir is underage, he is no different from a slave, although he owns the whole estate. The heir is subject to guardians and trustees until the time set by his father. So also, when we were underage, we were in slavery under the elemental spiritual forces of the world. But when the set time had fully come, God sent his Son, born of a woman, born under the law, to redeem those under the law, that we might receive adoption to sonship. Because you are his sons, God sent the Spirit of his Son into our hearts, the Spirit who calls out, 'Abba, Father.' So, you are no longer a slave, but God's child; and since you are his child, God has made you also an heir."*

Why did Jesus come into the world? To open the door for you to know that you are a child of God. He sent the Spirit of his Son into your heart, the Spirit who calls out, "Abba, Father." Jesus came to enable us to become children of God.

So, in Christ Jesus, you are all children of God through faith, for all of you who were baptized into Christ have clothed yourselves with Christ. Jesus is the door that gives us access to our Heavenly Father's heart. Faith is the key that unlocks the door. The word faith in Greek, pistis, means conviction, confidence, trust, belief, reliance, trustworthiness, and persuasion. In the New Testament setting, faith is the divinely implanted principle of inward confidence, assurance, trust, and reliance on God and all that He says. Faith is the key that unlocks the door—Jesus—which allows you to enter the Father's heart and to know Him as your loving, trustworthy Heavenly Father.

You may ask, "Am I worthy enough to become a child of God?" There is no discrimination with God in the adoption process. There is neither Jew nor Gentile, neither slave nor free, nor is there male and female, for you are all one in Christ Jesus. We live in a world of prejudice and discrimination. Not so in God's Kingdom. The heart of God is open to any who call on the name of the Lord Jesus Christ. Jesus came to share His inheritance with you through adoption into His family.

If you belong to Christ, then you are Abraham's seed, and heirs according to the promise. What the Apostle Paul is saying is that if an heir is underage, he is no different from a slave, although he owns the whole estate. The heir is subject to guardians and trustees until the time set by his father. So also, when we were underage, we were in slavery under the elemental spiritual forces of the world. Prior to being adopted into Jesus' family, you were a slave to sin and the world. Before Jesus came into your life, your inheritance was confined to the elemental forces of the world. But when the set time had fully come, God sent his Son, born of a woman, born under the law, to redeem those under the law, that we might receive adoption to sonship. Jesus opens the way for you to be adopted into His family to see God the Father as your Heavenly Father in whom you can always totally trust in all places with every aspect of your life. Adoption affords you all the rights, privileges, and benefits of a biological child.

Your inheritance in Christ Jesus is clearly spelled out by the Apostle Peter. 1 Peter 1:3-9 says,

> *"Praise be to the God and Father of our Lord Jesus Christ! In his great mercy he has given us new birth into a living hope through the resurrection of Jesus Christ from the dead, and into an inheritance that can never perish, spoil, or fade. This inheritance is kept in heaven for you, who through faith are shielded by God's power until the coming of the salvation that is ready to be revealed in the last time. In all this you greatly rejoice, though now for a little while you may have had to suffer grief in all kinds of trials. These have come so that the proven genuineness of your faith—of greater worth than gold, which perishes even though refined by fire—may result in praise, glory, and honor when Jesus Christ is revealed. Though you have not seen him, you love him; and even though you do not see him now, you believe in him and are filled with an inexpressible and glorious joy, for you are receiving the result of your faith, the salvation of your souls."*

What awaits you is beyond your imagination! The joys you experience in this life will be overshadowed a million times more by the inheritance that awaits you in Heaven as a child of the Living God. Some of you have had a wonderful relationship with your earthly father. That is awesome, and I am truly celebrating for you. But for those who have had a less than perfect relationship, there is hope for restoration through Jesus Christ when you are born again.

A friend of mine brought his wife to see me. They attended church on an intermittent basis, and both stated that they were Christians. He had pre-warned me that she was depressed and never seemed to have any joy in her life. After a lengthy discussion about many topics, I asked her if she had a good relationship with her father. She immediately looked away with a blank stare. I waited until she spoke. "He was a jerk!" she blurted followed by a long period of silence. Just as I started to probe, she launched a barrage of horrific tales about the way he had cheated on her mother multiple times, made promises to his children that he never kept, slowly drifted out of their collective lives until the day came when he just disappeared. Finally, she stopped talking and started sobbing. I asked her if I could speak for her earthly father. Reluctantly, she agreed. I walked her down the painful pathway of forgiveness for her father to lay him and all the bitterness, resentment, hate, anger, frustration at the foot of the cross. She gave and released it all until she had nothing more to let go of. I then placed my hand on her head and spoke for her father declaring a father's blessing over her. She appeared physically exhausted, but a peace came over her as she laid on my shoulder. Next, I asked her if I could speak for her Heavenly Father. She peered up at me with a confused look uncertain of what I meant. I said, close your eyes and listen to the voice of God. I then told her that God had never abandoned her and would never leave her. God loves her. God is proud of her. God calls her His beloved and she is His princess. And then I proclaimed for God in His most gentle voice, "Can you trust me?" She paused and said, "Yes!" I then prayed for an impartation of the Father's Love to be poured into her from above and fill every cell of her body with His love. The following Bible passages came to my mind in that moment:

> *Romans 5:5, "And hope does not put us to shame, because God's love has been poured out into our hearts through the Holy Spirit, who has been given to us."*

> *1 John 4:18, "There is no fear in love. But perfect love drives out fear because fear has to do with punishment. The one who fears is not made perfect in love."*

She smiled and said she felt peace and love like she had never known. The depression, sadness, and self-doubt, all the hate and rejection left her that day. Her demeanor changed. She became joyful and content. Her husband graciously thanked me, and I said, "Thank Jesus. He is the One who healed your wife." Once she was able to release the bitterness and forgive her father, she was open to the fullness of what her Heavenly father had supernaturally in store for her.

No matter how bad your circumstance was with your father, God can heal and restore you! Jesus said He came to make all things new (Revelation 21:5). This includes you. Let Him into your life as your Lord and Savior and you will become NEW!

Chapter Seven

DOROTHY'S STORY

The power of restoration can flow through God's beloved saints if they are willing to be used by Him. The following narrative is an uplifting story told by a dear layman friend of mine, Robert. He walked a woman through the process of forgiving her father and receiving the Father's Blessing:

Greetings. My name is Robert. I met Pastor Paul Teske and his wife Rivers about 13 years ago. Pastor Paul was here in Dallas, Texas doing a teaching on the Father's Blessing; and a friend of mine, Philip, wanted me to attend and so I did. Those few nights of study and prayer were incredibly freeing for me. This simple biblical teaching of the Father's Blessing has changed my life and revolutionized the way that I see my Heavenly Father and His children. I will forever be indebted to Pastor Paul and Rivers for the amazing teaching that they gave away for free. But that is how it is in the kingdom; our Father gives to us freely and wants us to share with others what He has given us. And with that said, I want to tell you about an extraordinary event that occurred in the life of my mother-in-law, Dorothy, that helped to set her free to live for God the best that she could. It started with a blessing from her Father.

Dorothy was going through a separation with her third husband, David, at the time and struggling to understand how this could happen to her again. Dorothy was surrounded by a family that loved the Lord, and she had confessed as a young person to a saving relationship with the Lord Jesus Christ; but still found herself struggling spiritually. Distant from the church, not active in the community and plagued by many health issues, Dorothy was feeling alone and distant from the Father.

As I know much of the story now, I understand why she was feeling this way. When Dorothy was 19 years old, she got pregnant out of wedlock. In the 1960s, it was frowned upon by her family, especially her father, Colin. On the night that Dorothy and her future husband, William, came to tell her parents of her pregnancy, her father and William got into a fight. The resulting fight ended with her father breaking William's arm. Then her father commenced to tell the family that he was leaving and divorcing her mother, Betty. Talk about things going from bad to worse. And the feeling that you not only disappointed your mother and father, but that you could have been the cause for the destruction of your family unit. What a weight to bear for the rest of your life! Moving forward, your own sisters would harbor great resentment toward your father and thus maybe even you for the rest of your life.

As sad as this may sound, Dorothy still loved her father and wanted to remember him fondly. Anytime the family got together, however, Colin was spoken of poorly and with much contempt. I have been a part of this family for more than 20 years. There are grandchildren who have no recollection of their grandfather but speak as if he were the essence of evil for divorcing their grandmother, Betty. Dorothy sat in silence at these family gatherings for years, taking in the disdain for her father, wondering if she was partly to blame for the wreckage.

When Dorothy and David finally separated, I began to spend more time with her: helping with chores around her house and bringing my kids over to hang out and see their grandmother. Oftentimes, we would begin to discuss things of the Lord. Dorothy would ask me questions, and I would open my Bible and we would talk for what would seem like hours. During these times, the Holy Spirit began to weigh upon my heart that Dorothy needed something. It was also during this time period that I had met Pastor Paul. I learned long ago that there are no coincidences. The Lord Jesus has you where you are and learning what you are learning for a right-now purpose.

I asked my wife if she thought that her mother would be receptive to the Father's Blessing. My wife, Tina, said that it did not need to be me who gave the blessing but could Philip, our friend, come to our house and do it. I thought that was a great idea and contacted Philip to make arrangements. My wife contacted her mom and asked if she would like to come over and meet a friend of ours. I think she was a little vague at the time so that we would not scare Dorothy away. But all parties agreed to a Saturday morning meeting.

One of the things that Pastor Paul teaches is that we have to invite the Holy Spirit into what we are doing. We must give the Holy Spirit the welcome to be there, as well as we must have a sense of expectation and faith that the Holy Spirit will do what Jesus said: leading and guiding us into all truth. It only takes the faith of a mustard seed, and sometimes that is all we have. So, my wife and I began to pray with expectation for Saturday, knowing that our Father would do something wonderful.

On Saturday, the four of us gathered together in our living room. Never one to waste time, Philip began to invite and pray for the Holy Spirit to come into the room and bring his life-giving presence. Philip began to ask Dorothy some questions. Did your father Colin ever tell you he loved you? Did he ever bless you as his daughter? Dorothy said that her father had told her he loved her but had never given her a blessing. Philip then explained that this is a right for the children of the Lord to receive a blessing.

This is the part where the Lord stepped in. Philip asked Dorothy if she would like to receive a blessing from her father, the kind of blessing that a good father would give to his daughter if he knew how? Dorothy's father, Colin, had passed away many years before this; I thought that she might have been a little skeptical at the time. But now, with eyes filled with tears, she said "yes" she would like that. So Philip stood over Dorothy and began to anoint her head with oil. Then he laid his hand on her head and said that the Father in Heaven and her earthly father, if he were able, wanted to give her a blessing today. As Philip continued, he said, "Dorothy, I am standing in the place of your Father today, and I want you to know that I love you, and that I bless you today; and that I want you to know that everything in your life is going to be okay." At this point my mother-in-law let out a wailing cry of relief. It was as if years of sadness and frustration came out at that moment. She stood and embraced Philip for a very long moment, and He as the Father's representative embraced her back. And to me it looked as if the two of them were surrounded in God's glorious light. It looked like a father and his daughter long separated from one another but finally reunited and whole.

I cannot say that everything changed in that moment for

Dorothy; but watching her life for the next 13 years, I know that something happened. And that something is this: Dorothy began to walk closely with her Heavenly Father after that day. She began by reading and studying the Bible. She became a regular church attendee. She volunteered at the local hospital as the "popcorn lady." She began to give her time to the local elementary school helping children to read and giving them that extra help and love that many children need. Most surprising is that she would make regular appointments with her pastor just to talk and be an encouragement to him. She would go on to live a life of joyous giving with all the time she had.

My mother-in-law, Dorothy, went home to be with the Lord on March 31, 2021. Her services were a celebration of life and left those of us that loved her with an amazing peace that passes all understanding. Even in death, she still was a giver of life and a blessing to those around her, like our Lord Jesus. She donated her body to science and, as a result of that gift, was able to give so much more to others and help better their lives. At the writing of this story, my wife and her family are receiving letters and thank you cards from those who received her donations. I think that Dorothy knew that she was loved and, most importantly, she knew that her Heavenly Father loved her.

Chapter Eight

THREE STEPS TO RESTORATION

Do you want your father wound healed by receiving the Father's Blessing? If so, then I believe the time has arrived for a supernatural intervention by the Living God. I can assure you that receiving the Father's Blessing will transform your life. The power of God's love poured into every cell of your body will wash away fear, doubt, anxiety, and despair.

> *Romans 5:5, "And hope does not put us to shame, because God's love has been poured out into our hearts through the Holy Spirit, who has been given to us."*

What do you need to do to receive this divine intervention?

1. Forgive your earthly father(s)
2. Trust your Heavenly Father
3. Receive an impartation of the Father's love

Step 1: Forgive your earthly father

Some of you have or had a wonderful relationship with your earthly father. That is awesome, and I celebrate with you. However, many of you did not have a stellar relationship with your father, which has created a dilemma in your life.

Maybe your father never told you that he loved you.

Maybe you never knew your father.

Maybe he never:

- Hugged you
- Affirmed you
- Encouraged you
- Supported you
- Blessed you
- Maybe he was:
- Physically absent
- Emotionally absent
- Verbally abusive
- Physically abusive
- Sexually abusive

Maybe you are harboring toward him:

- Unforgiveness
- Bitterness
- Resentment
- Frustration
- Anger
- Rejection

There may be other things that come to mind as you think about the relationship you had or have with your father. Regardless of how bad your relationship was, you need to forgive him and release him to God. Therein lies your choice. If you do not forgive and let go of these negative feelings, you will continue to be held emotionally captive to him whether he is alive or dead. These ill feelings—and they are truly ill—are robbing you of emotional health and wholeness. I know that this is difficult, but do you want to be held in bondage to these feelings any longer, or do you want to be free?

Several years ago, I ministered to a businessman in his mid-50s who played his cards very close to his vest. He trusted no one. At first, he was understandably distant at our introduction but, after a few minutes of conversation, his defenses slowly dissipated. I asked him about his relationship with his father, which was not good. To complicate things, he said that he was still grieving the loss of a child who had died years earlier. We talked about that tragic life-changing event for quite a while. After he finished, I asked him if I could pray with him. He gave me an affirmative nod. I led him through a prayer for his broken heart. I assured him that his child was in Heaven waiting to be reunited with him for all eternity. He found incredible peace in knowing that he would see his child again. We then addressed his father issues and some of the painful memories that he had encountered growing up, which had bitterly extended into his adult years. I asked him if I could speak for his father. He agreed. I spoke as his father, confessing all the wrong that I had done and apologized. I then asked for his forgiveness. Initially, he pushed back, but eventually said that he forgave his father for everything and released him to the Lord. He then admitted that he had resented God for taking his child. I told him that God had never turned His back on him and would never abandon him. I asked him if he could trust God with this life going forward and he said yes. I then prayed for an impartation of the Father's love to fill him completely and thoroughly in his entire body. I blessed him as his surrogate father and spoke a blessing over him from his Heavenly Father.

He could not wait to gather his family together to share the breakthrough he had experienced and to apologize for his utter failure in telling them how much he loved them, how proud he was of them, and all that he wanted to share from lost years. Then he made a commitment that he would place his hands on each of them individually and bless his children with the Father's Blessing. He followed up with me the next week to let me know what had transpired. He said he verbally addressed the issue of over achievement and setting such unrealistic expectations on the entire family and asked for their forgiveness. He also laid his hands on each child and blessed them. He said the entire family was in shock and thought it was a true miracle that their father had shared honestly from his heart and committed to change as a father and husband. They cried together and each child melted in his arms as he hugged them. He started going to church with his family and has never looked back.

This is an awesome testimony of how forgiving an earthly father clears the pathway to receive the Heavenly Father's Blessing.

The Spiritual Preparation to Receive

If you do not know Jesus Christ as your personal Savior, and want to settle this issue right how in your heart, then pray to God the Father:

- Repent of your sin
- Confess your faith in Jesus Christ as your Lord and Savior who died on the cross for your sin and rose from the grave to give you everlasting life
- Ask Jesus to fill you with the Holy Spirit
- Amend your life to live to the Glory of God

As a believer in the Triune God—Father, Son and Holy Spirit—use the ancient words of the Apostles' Creed, which clearly expresses the basic tenets of the Christian faith, and follow this profession of faith by praying the Lord's Prayer.

The Apostles Creed

I believe in God the Father almighty,
    maker of heaven and earth.
    I believe in Jesus Christ, His only Son, our Lord,
    Who was conceived by the Holy Spirit
    born of the Virgin Mary.
    He suffered under Pontius Pilate,
    was crucified, died and buried;
    he descended to hell.

The third day He rose again from the dead.

He ascended into Heaven
and sits on the right hand of God the Father Almighty.
From there He shall come to judge the living and the dead.

I believe in the Holy Spirit,
    the Holy Christian Church,
    the Communion of Saints,
    the Forgiveness of sins,
    the Resurrection of the body,
    and the life everlasting. Amen.

The Lord's Prayer

Our Father in heaven,
hallowed be your name,
your kingdom come,
your will be done,
on earth as in heaven.
Give us today our daily bread.
Forgive us our sins as we forgive those who sin against us.
Save us from the time of trial, and deliver us from evil.
For the kingdom, the power, and the glory are yours,
now and forever. Amen.

Make a list of everything you need to forgive your father for:

You can call upon the Holy Spirit to help bring to your remembrance all that needs to be laid at the cross.

If I could personally walk this out one-on-one with you, I would ask you to tell me your father's name. I would then take you in my arms and hold you close to my chest and tell you that I am going to speak for your father, as though it was him holding you and speaking into your ear. Although we are not physically together, I have seen this work wonderfully with individuals over the phone or in large event settings. Remember, God is not restricted by time or space. He knows all your anguish. This will be a supernatural intervention from heaven to your heart. God's Word—written or spoken—never goes forth without having a miraculous impact. I believe this Isaiah passage is applicable for you.

> *Isaiah 55:10-11, "As the rain and the snow come down from Heaven, and do not return to it without watering the earth and making it bud and flourish, so that it yields seed for the sower and bread for the eater, so is my word that goes out from my mouth: It will not return to me empty, but will accomplish what I desire and achieve the purpose for which I sent it."*

So, keep going:

- Capture a mental picture of your father (maybe you have a photograph of him to hold and look at)
- Close your eyes and listen to his voice. Open the ears of your heart
- Let me speak for your earthly father right now
- If possible, have your mentor or father-figure or clergyman speak these words to you while he embraces you

"I am sincerely sorry from the bottom of my heart for…"

- Never saying "I Love You"
- Never telling you how proud I am of you
- Never telling you how important you are to me
- Never telling you_____
- Never blessing you
- Dismissing you
- Minimizing your pain
- Never hugging you
- Abandoning you
- Aloofness
- Dismissing you when you needed me
- Cruelty
- Abuse in any form:
  - Sexual
  - Physical
  - Mental
  - Verbal

- Negligence
- Shaming
- Disappearing
- Dying before I could reconcile with you
- Alienation
- Not being there when you needed me

- Not celebrating with you the important milestones of your life
  - Birth
  - Graduation
  - Special events
  - Wedding
  - Your Children
  - _____

- I am so sorry.

"I am so ashamed of the way I mistreated you..."

- Injured you
- Hurt you
- Harmed you
- Neglected you
- Abused you
- Violated you

"If I could erase the past and start over I would..."

- Change everything that hurt you
- Take back every word that hurt you
- Undo every broken promise I made to you
- Attend every event of your life
- Hold you. Hug you
- Tell you over and over how much I love you, how proud

of you I am, how happy I am that you are mine

- How special you are to me, you are my beloved, my prince/princess
- I would rest my hands on your head and give you my Father's Blessing
- Please forgive me for anything that I did to hurt you

Pause: At this point, you may feel as though you can forgive your father. Then do so and continue.

On the other hand, you may be feeling overwhelmed with a variety of negative emotions, and the thought of forgiving him seems impossible. If you have hit an emotional roadblock at this juncture, then I want you to return to the beginning of this chapter and ask the Lord to give you the strength, courage, and guidance not to give up!

"If you can forgive me, then I want to thank you"

- Thank you
- I bless you as my beloved child. I love you. I am proud of you.

Step Two: Trust your Heavenly Father

"Now I want to speak for your Heavenly Father…"

- I know your heartache and pain. I know what you have been through
- I heard your sobbing through the night as I stood by

your bed

- I collected all your tears
- I want you to know that I have never left your side—day or night
- I have always been with you when you endured those hardships, heartaches, and abuse
- I have never taken my eyes off you
- I will never abandon you nor turn my back on you
- There is nothing you could ever do to separate my eternal love from you
- I love you
- I am proud of you
- You are my beloved
- You are my child, my prince/princess
- Can you trust me? Trust me with your life?
- I bless you with a heavenly father's blessing which is irrevocable, sealed by the Holy Spirit

Step Three: Receive an impartation of the Father's Love

Father God, I pray right now that You would release a full impartation of Your love into Your beloved child [Your Name] now in the name of Jesus. Soak every cell in his/her body with Your divine love, peace, hope, joy, and faith. Refresh, restore, and revive him/her now!

Father in Heaven, I pray Romans 5:5 over your dear child

[Speak Your Name] that you would pour out your love by the Holy Spirit into his/her heart. Fill him/her up. Let his/her cup overflow.

> *Romans 5:5, "And hope does not put us to shame, because God's love has been poured out into our hearts through the Holy Spirit, who has been given to us."*

I declare Your promise spoken in Romans 8:37-39 over their present and future that you will never abandon Your beloved child.

> *Romans 8:37-39, "No, in all these things we are more than conquerors through Him who loved us. For I am convinced that neither death nor life, neither angels nor demons, neither the present nor the future, nor any powers, neither height nor depth, nor anything else in all creation, will be able to separate us from the love of God that is in Christ Jesus our Lord."*

I know that God answers prayer. I pray that He will meet you in this moment and transform your life.

> *Psalm 37:3-6, "Trust in the Lord and do good; dwell in the land and enjoy safe pasture. Take delight in the Lord, and He will give you the desires of your heart. Commit your way to the Lord; trust in Him and He will do this: He will make your righteous reward shine like the dawn, your vindication like the*

noonday sun."

Amen!

Congratulations! You've completed your personal journey through this arduous process. I know it was plagued with painful memories, moments of denial, considerations to cancel, and a variety of other reflections and thoughts about the uncertainty of outcome. But you finished. You gave your burdens to God, and He took them ALL away.

> *Psalm 55:22, "Cast your cares on the Lord and he will sustain you; he will never let the righteous be shaken."*
>
> *1 Peter 5:7, "Cast all your anxiety on him because he cares for you."*

I want you to thank God for His mercy, love, grace, forgiveness, and peace. You are free from the emotional heartache of your past. You are God's beloved in whom He is well pleased.

This is the start of your new life, free of the pain of yesterday. I want you to know that this is a new beginning for you spiritually, emotionally, mentally, relationally, and physically. God is with you and will never forsake you. Going forward, I want you to begin every day with the Lord in prayer, read His Word (the Bible) and find a suitable mentor to walk with you as a guide and encourager. You will have down moments, but never look back—always be a forward-looking person.

EPILOGUE

I began diligently anointing the sick with oil and praying for healing in 1994. Over the course of the next ten years, I saw four people miraculously healed. Regardless of the infinitesimal amount of healing—one every two and a half years—I felt compelled to continue to pray for healing. Then God shook my paradigm. On May 7, 2004, while speaking to two hundred businessmen at the New Canaan Society in Connecticut, I suffered a cerebral hemorrhage, which immediately paralyzed my left side. While in the hospital, God spoke to me and told me that I would be healed in twenty-one days. Upon leaving the hospital in a wheelchair, I was told by the medical staff that, even after physical therapy, I would need to wear a leg brace for the rest of my life. The medical community could do nothing to restore me. They were done, but NOT GOD!

Twenty-one days after my stroke, Rivers drove me to Baltimore to attend a large healing crusade. On that Friday night, exactly as the Lord had promised, I was completely healed during worship. No one prayed for me or laid hands on me; I was instantly healed during worship. Without any knowledge of my condition of paralysis or that I had been healed, the minister leading the service called Rivers and me to the platform to receive a healing and deliverance ministry. I told him that I had arrived paralyzed, and that God had completely healed me. He then declared that thousands of people would be healed by Jesus through our ministry.

Since my healing on May 28, 2004, Rivers and I have traveled to teach and minister in over seventy countries on six continents in venues including: healing crusades in large stadiums; teaching, demonstrating, and imparting the gifts we received to others in churches, camp meetings and homes; television and radio; seminars; as well as teaching in bible schools, seminaries and colleges. In addition, we have witnessed thousands give their lives to Jesus as He confirmed the Gospel with signs, wonders, and miracles. God convicted me to take the gift He had given Rivers and me and give it away.

> *Matthew 10:8, "Heal the sick, raise the dead, cleanse those who have leprosy, drive out demons. Freely you have received; freely give."*

I have witnessed many miraculous healings in my ministry since my healing in 2004. The following list is but a few:

- A young Baptist pastor's wife in Charleston in a wheelchair with paralyzed legs following the birth of her fourth child stands up and walks out of the meeting leaving the wheelchair behind

- A woman with a severe nut allergy in Daytona Beach instantly healed.

- A man in Chicago with incurable Trigeminal Neuralgia (Mayo Clinic calls it the "suicide disease") healed

- A woman in Minneapolis with inoperable, incurable liver cancer healed

- A blind Presbyterian woman healed

- A woman in Illinois with Meniere's Disease instantly healed

- A seventeen-year-old girl, a "cutter"—severely depressed and heavily medicated—instantly healed

- A twelve-year-old girl with incurable cancer in Connecticut healed

- A seventeen-year-old girl in Dallas with multiple tumors in her lungs healed

- An eighteen-year-old man in Little Rock with Tourette's instantly healed

- An eighteen-month-old baby in Canada with a flaming esophagus instantly healed

Why do I share these miracles with you? I want you to understand that with God, all things are possible. If God can raise us from the dead, then He can heal and restore any disease that assaults you. God can heal your heart, memories, and relationships.

> *Psalm 103:2-3, "Praise the Lord, my soul, and forget not all his benefits—who forgives all your sins and heals all your diseases."*

This includes the complete restoration of your broken heart. I have often said that it is easier to pray for a broken leg than a broken heart. However, I believe that your Heavenly Father has given you a new heart and is going to walk hand-in-hand with you the rest of your life. He loves you. He will never abandon you. You are His best creative gift!

I want to share DAILY spiritual exercises for you to maintain your healing as you walk with the Lord. I encourage everyone who has experienced a personal healing from God (emotional, relational, physical and/or spiritual) to walk out these spiritual steps to reinforce their faith. Please, for your sake, commit to do these spiritual steps to maintain your healing:

1. Worship God

   John 4:23-24, "Yet a time is coming and has now come when the true worshipers will worship the Father in the Spirit and in truth, for they are the kind of worshipers the Father seeks. God is spirit, and his worshipers must worship in the Spirit and in truth."

2. Fellowship with Christians

   1 Thessalonians 5:11, "Therefore encourage one another and build each other up, just as in fact you are doing."

3. Read the Bible

   Psalm 1:2, "But whose delight is in the law of the Lord, and who meditates on his law day and night."

4. Pray Constantly

   1 Thessalonians 5:16-18, "Rejoice always, pray continually, give thanks in all circumstances; for this is

God's will for you in Christ Jesus."

5. Take Holy Communion

Luke 22:19-20, "And he took bread, gave thanks and broke it, and gave it to them, saying, 'This is my body given for you; do this in remembrance of me.' In the same way, after the supper he took the cup, saying, 'This cup is the new covenant in my blood, which is poured out for you.'"

1 Corinthians 11:28-29, "Everyone ought to examine themselves before they eat of the bread and drink from the cup. For those who eat and drink without discerning the body of Christ eat and drink judgment on themselves."

6. Share your Healing Story

Revelation 12:11, "They triumphed over him by the blood of the Lamb and by the word of their testimony; they did not love their lives so much as to shrink from death."

7. Put on the Armor of God

Ephesians 6:11, "Put on the full armor of God, so that you can take your stand against the devil's schemes."

I believe that if you make a daily commitment to reinforce your faith with these steps at a minimum, you will stay the course of health and wholeness through the Power of the Holy Spirit embedded in you as His Temple. Jesus Christ has redeemed you and your Heavenly Father loves you too much to ever let go of you.

I want to encourage you to make a list of other Bible passages that come to mind and journal them for your daily review and time with God.

I want to speak a Father's Blessing over you which is taken from the Old and New Testament.

> *Heavenly Father, I speak as a spiritual father over your beloved child, redeemed by the blood of Christ and sanctified by the Holy Spirit, and bless her/him with a Father's Blessing that you spoke over your people.*
>
> *Numbers 6:22-27, "The Lord said to Moses, Tell Aaron and his sons, this is how you are to bless the Israelites. Say to them: The Lord bless you and keep you; the Lord make his face shine on you and be gracious to you; the Lord turn his face toward you and give you peace. So, they will put my name on the Israelites, and I will bless them."*
>
> *2 Corinthians 13:14, "May the grace of the Lord Jesus Christ, and the love of God, and the fellowship of the Holy Spirit be with you all."*

Remember, you are your Father's favorite—His beloved! Go in

peace and serve the Lord.

MY FATHER

My father, Raymond H. C. Teske Sr. was born on January 30, 1917, in Chicago Illinois to Herman Teske and Alva Seraphia Teske (nee Lundmark) and would be their only child. He was born into what would become known as The Greatest Generation. His parents initially lived with my father's grandparents who had been immigrants from Germany during the mid-1800s. My grandfather was a bookbinder by profession and my grandmother worked for the telephone company. They eventually bought a modest home in Lincoln Park . My grandfather struggled with alcoholism. The stories abounded about how my drunken grandfather would come home in the early morning hours and battle with my grandmother. My young father would try to separate them only to be beaten along with his mother who would then walk the streets until my grandfather passed out and it would be safe for mother and child to return home.

My grandparents were divorced when my father was sixteen years old. My grandmother raised my dad as a single mom without much help from family. She made a decent wage while my father was able to attend college and play football in Chicago during the depression years. He had a car and was hired by an uncle with a small business in the late 1930s. When World War II began, my father joined the 106 Black Horse Cavalry, which his uncles had joined during the Great War. He was sent to Louisiana for training before being deployed to Europe.

His unit trained at Camp Livingston near Monroe, Louisiana. One weekend he was given a pass to attend a small Lutheran church in Monroe where he met, courted, and married my mother within a few months, much to his mother's chagrin. Before he went to England in preparation for the invasion of Europe, my older brother was born. Finally the time arrived for him to go to war, leaving my mother and brother in Monroe with her parents.

My dad boarded a ship for the D-Day invasion of June 6, 1944. While crossing the English Channel, his transport ship hit a mine, and the damaged ship was ordered to return to England. His outfit was delayed a few days but, eventually, made the crossing to Normandy. If he had landed on D-Day, I may not be here to tell my story. In 1972 as a Lutheran seminary graduate student in Germany, I visited the Omaha and Utah Beaches of Normandy where the allied forces landed. It was a poignant day for me, to say the least.

After crossing France, Germany, and pushing into Austria in 1945, his cavalry unit was delayed for six months while protecting the King of Belgium from his own people. The people of Belgium were enraged because of his passive surrender to the Nazis and wanted to kill him. Eventually, my dad's unit returned stateside in December 1945, and I was born in early October of 1946. I am in the first wave of the postwar baby group called the Boomers. My dad returned to Monroe where he went to work for the local newspaper. After the birth of my first sister, he moved the family to Waco, TX, to work for the local newspaper in 1950 where he was employed until he retired in 1982. My parents had one more daughter.

My father was active in the local Lutheran church and was a very devout man. He served as Scoutmaster of Troop 36 where my brother and I both made the rank of Eagle Scout. Our lives were full and busy with activities making sure we went hunting, fishing, and camping every chance we had. He bought us each a 410-gauge shotgun on our eighth birthday. He poured himself into our lives. I believe that he had made an agreement with God that if he were to survive the war, he would dedicate his life to God, country, and to his family. He tried to be the father that he never had. He hugged us, told us that he loved us and was proud of us. He called me "Admiral" until he died. (I served as a Navy Chaplain for 20 years—I would have loved to have the retirement check of an admiral, but did not quite make it!)

My dad died on March 23, 2005. While attending his funeral, I thought about my Grandfather Teske's funeral in 1962 in Chicago. It was held in a local funeral home. The brief service and graveside ritual were conducted by a young Lutheran pastor. I remember several relatives with my grandmother and our family as the few in attendance. I also remember my dad's somber face and believe his sadness was coupled with a sense of remorse. In sharp contrast, my mind suddenly transitioned back to my dad's funeral. My deep sadness at his loss was protected with fond memories. My father gave me those memories and, for that, I am forever grateful.

All things said and done, I believe the impact of the dysfunctional family system he was raised in helped him rise above his hurt and troubled memories to generously give his children unconditional love and affirmation that he never knew as a son. He certainly modeled fatherhood for me and my siblings in an incredibly positive way. My dad was not perfect, and neither am I, but I believe he did the best he could to verbally affirm us. My father never received a father's blessing, but he blessed his children.

I have tried to pass the life lessons on to my own children—and, now, grandchildren—that I received from a faithful man, my dad. I affectionately tell my children and grandchildren daily that I love them, am proud of them, and affirm all that they have become either in-person or through the gift of social media. I hug them when I can, and I have placed my hands on their heads to bless them with a father's blessing. Why? Because it blesses me to impart a father's blessing to them knowing it is critical and biblical to do so. Amen!

ABOUT THE AUTHOR

Pastor Paul Teske was ordained into the Lutheran Church/Missouri Synod and married to Rivers Hatchett in 1976. He served twenty years as a Navy Chaplain and thirty years in parish ministry. Rivers and Paul have traveled to seventy countries on six continents with a global healing ministry. He is an author, speaker and oversees a world-wide social media ministry. Rivers and Paul currently reside in their home state of Texas where he serves as Pastor Emeritus.

SOCIAL MEDIA

Paul Teske Ministries

Facebook, Instagram, YouTube

www.paulteskeministries.com

Rev222 *nonprofit ministry*

www.rev222.org

Hidden Choices comprehensively serves the individual, the family, the community by aggressively meeting the deepest emerging needs of children and women specifically in the United States, India and Africa at this time. As an organization, we are continually and aggressively seeking and vetting viable organizations which are committed to meeting the needs with sustainable resources and tools that empower and give life; whereby, building future citizens that are equipped to lead. By financially funding and supporting these organizations through our initiatives and those of our partners, we are making the difference in our global family by effectively saving millions of lives and changing the world in which we live.

Learn more at HIDDENCHOICES.ORG

Rivers Teske founded Hidden Choices, Inc. as an international nonprofit organization in supporting young women and children living in extreme crisis and poverty. It was while living and working in Asia during the 1980's and 90's that she was moved to make a profound and passionate difference in the lives of people who were abandoned, hungry or discarded as "the world's throwaways." Today, Ms. Teske speaks Internationally and builds collaborative relationships with organizations and individuals who are intentional 21st century world changers.

She believes significant change can be made in today's global community through social investing and creative human possibility. Her passion is to alleviate extreme poverty through collaborative efforts in education which support the most vulnerable. Ms. Teske believes in the declared human rights of the family protected at all stages, achieving success and living life defined by purpose and love.

Learn more at

RIVERSTESKE.COM *and* STOPTHEWARONCHILDREN.COM

RESOURCES

Rivers Wanted

Does God Still Speak Today? Extraordinary Dreams and Visions from God to Encourage Your Life

RIVERS TESKE

Available on Amazon, Kindle, iBooks, Nook, Kobo & more.

Healing *for* TODAY

PAUL TESKE

Available on Amazon, Kindle, iBooks, Nook, Kobo & more.

Made in the USA
Las Vegas, NV
06 October 2022

56669825R00070